HMH | into Reading™

W9-AAS-305

my Book

Grade 3

Modules 1-5

Authors and Advisors

Alma Flor Ada • Kylene Beers • F. Isabel Campoy
Joyce Armstrong Carroll • Nathan Clemens
Anne Cunningham • Martha C. Hougen • Tyrone C. Howard
Elena Izquierdo • Carol Jago • Erik Palmer
Robert E. Probst • Shane Templeton • Julie Washington

Contributing Consultants

David Dockterman • Jill Eggleton

Printed in the U.S.A.

ISBN   978-0-358-46153-1

3 4 5 6 7 8 9 10   0029   29 28 27 26 25 24 23 22 21

4500826597

r1.21

Welcome to myBook!

Do you like to read different kinds of texts for all kinds of reasons? Do you have a favorite genre or author? What can you learn from a video? Do you think carefully about what you read and view?

Here are some tips to get the MOST out of what you read and view:

Set a Purpose. What is the title? What is the genre? What do you want to learn from this text or video? What about it looks interesting to you?

Read and Annotate. As you read, underline and highlight important words and ideas. Make notes about things you want to figure out or remember. What questions do you have? What are your favorite parts? Write them down!

Make Connections. How does the text or video connect to what you already know? To other texts or videos? To your own life or community? Talk to others about your ideas. Listen to their ideas, too.

Wrap It Up! Look back at your questions and annotations. What did you like best? What did you learn? What do you still want to know? How will you find out?

As you read the texts and watch the videos in this book, make sure you get the MOST out of them by using the tips above.

But, don't stop there . . . Decide what makes you curious, find out more about it, have fun, and never stop learning!

Module 1

What a Character!

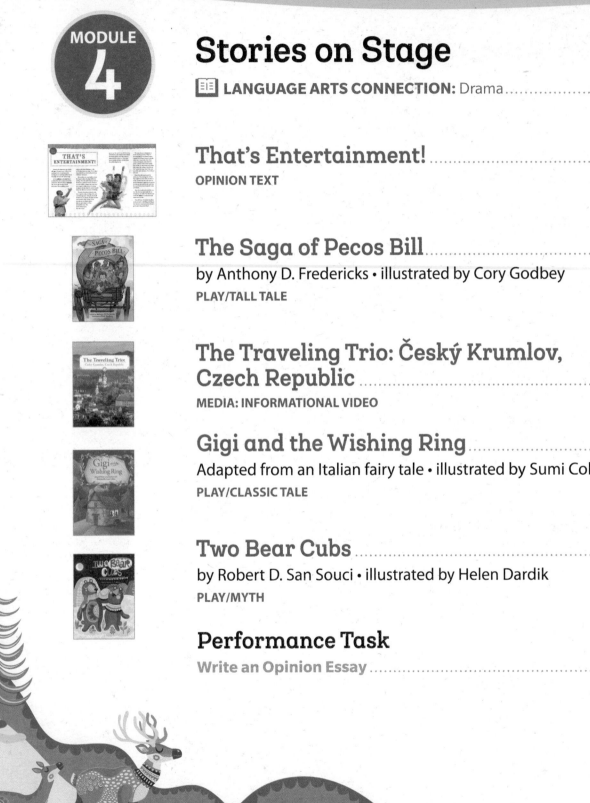

MODULE 4

Stories on Stage

📖 **LANGUAGE ARTS CONNECTION:** Drama

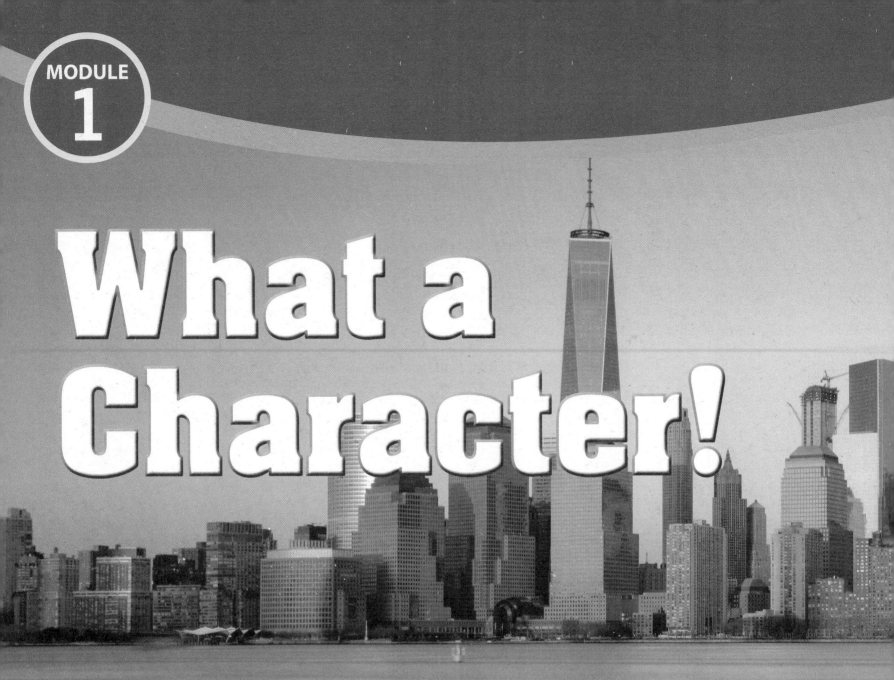

What a Character!

"Be true to yourself. Make
each day a masterpiece."
— John Wooden

What makes a character interesting?

Get Curious
▶ Video

Knowledge Map

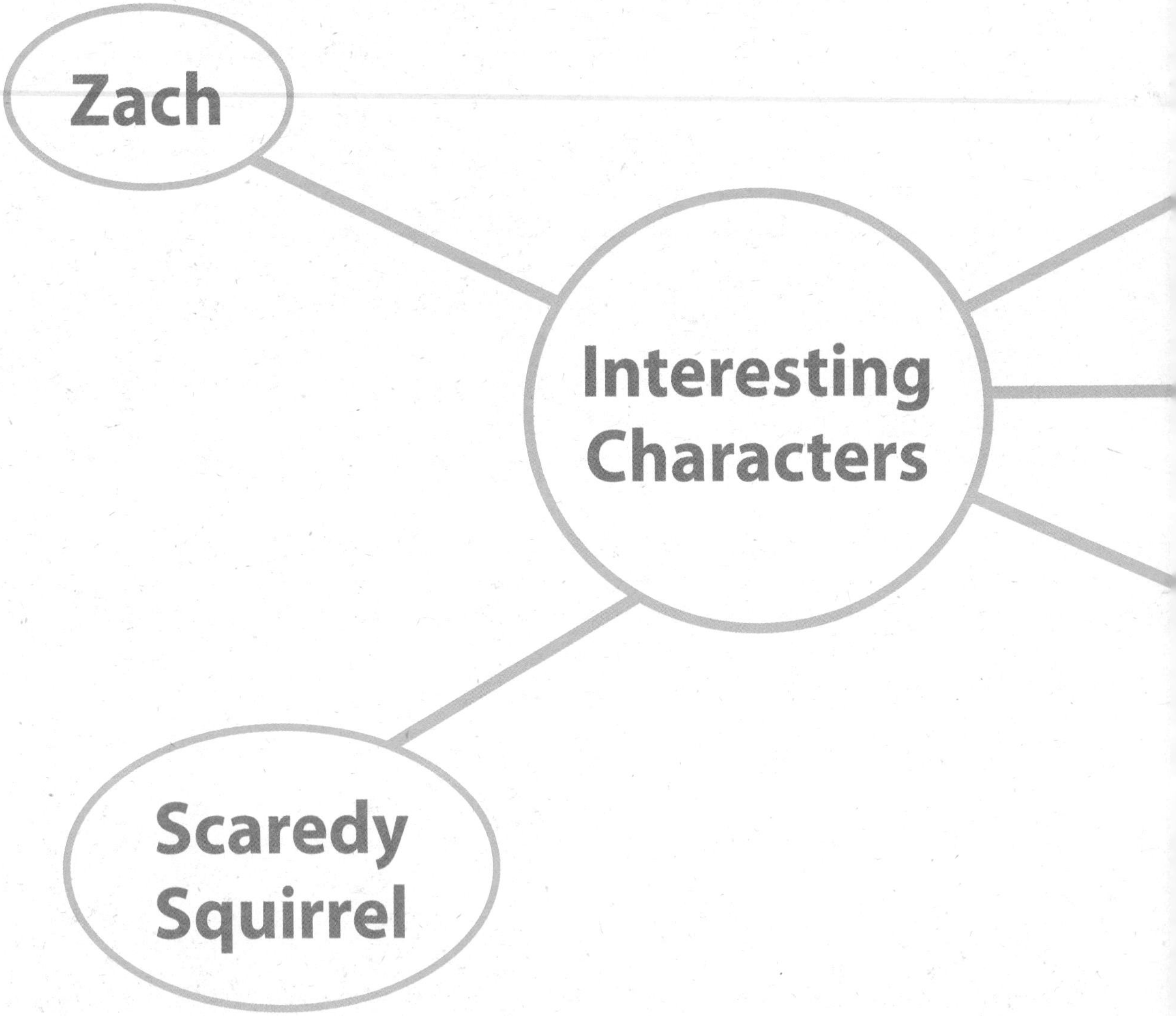
Zach
Interesting Characters
Scaredy Squirrel

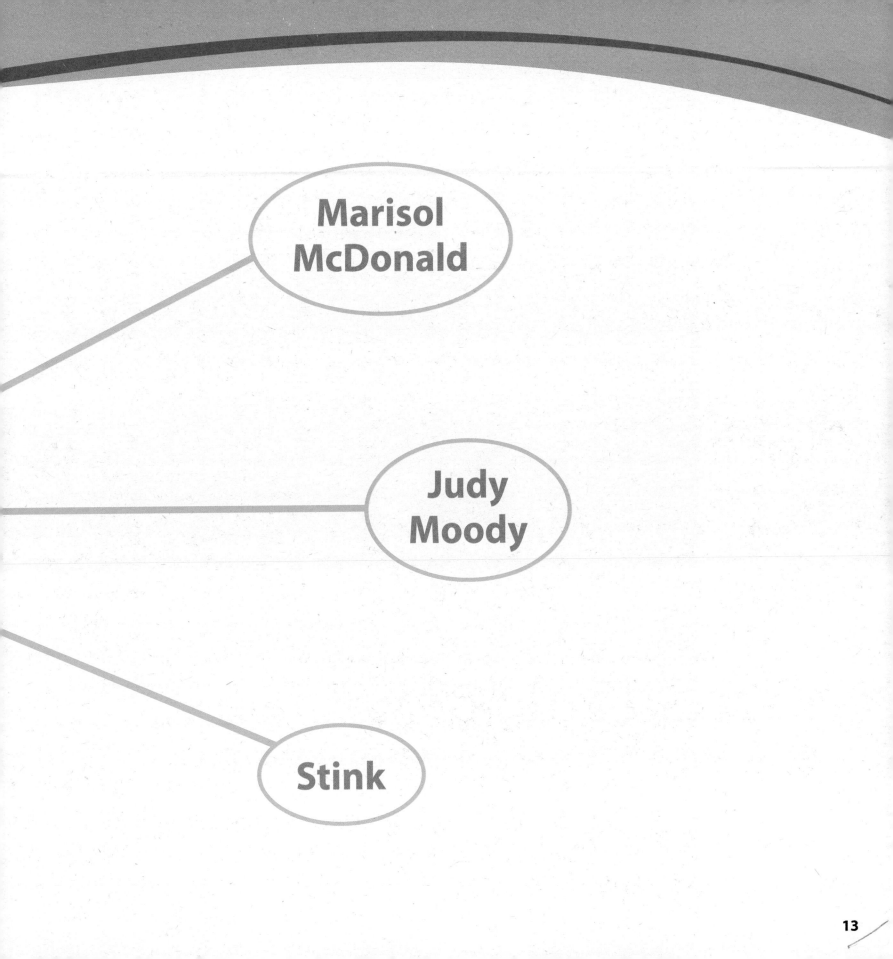

Marisol McDonald

Judy Moody

Stink

myNotes

Zach Jumps In!

1 My big brother Zach is a unique guy. There is no one like Zach. Most people admire him because he's such a strong athlete, but I admire him because he worked really hard to become one. You see, Zach is an amazing swimmer. Not just a fast or strong swimmer, but a champion swimmer. His ability is especially unusual because Zach was once terrified of the water!

2 When Zach was five, he fell into our neighbor's swimming pool. The water wasn't over his head. Still, he was REALLY scared. Mom quickly pulled Zach out of the pool. He was fine, but after that day, he hated the water.

3 Then Zach went to summer camp when he was ten. By that time, he loved sports. He was an excellent baseball and basketball player. He was very competitive and practiced a lot. That might be a main feature of Zach's personality. He always wants to win.

4 The one sport Zach couldn't win in was swimming. He was too afraid of the water to learn how. It made him mad that he was afraid.

5 So Zach made a plan. He needed a little help from a counselor named Trip. Each day, Trip took Zach to the lake, and each day, Zach inched toward the water. One day he finally put in one toe. The next day he put in his whole foot. In a week, he had walked in up to his knees! Then Zack did the bravest thing he had ever done. He jumped right in!

6 Zach likes to show his individuality by doing things differently. No camper had ever gone from not knowing how to swim to being a camp champion. Zach did that. He practiced and practiced. By the end of the summer, he won the camp swim meet. After that summer, Zach joined the swim team at his school. He's been swimming in competitions ever since.

7 Now Zach thinks there is nothing he can't do. He said his next challenge is to dive from the highest diving board. Oh, brother!

Internal
Personality Traits
- unique
- brave
- competitive
- determined

External
Physical Traits
- athletic
- strong

Zach

Challenges
- overcoming fears
- learning new skills
- doing things differently

Prepare to Read

GENRE STUDY **Realistic fiction** tells a story about characters and events that are like those in real life.

- Authors of realistic fiction include a plot with a conflict and resolution.
- Realistic fiction includes a setting, or a place and time, that is important to the story and characters who act, think, and speak like real people.
- Realistic fiction may include a theme or lesson learned by the characters.

SET A PURPOSE **Think about** the title and genre of this text. What do you think Marisol will do or say? How might she act? Write your ideas.

CRITICAL VOCABULARY

clash

winking

suggest

scrunches

mushy

usual

bilingual

mismatched

**Meet the Author and Illustrator:
Monica Brown and Sara Palacios**

Marisol McDonald Doesn't Match

Story by
Monica Brown

Illustrations by
Sara Palacios

1 **M**y name is Marisol McDonald, and I don't match. At least, that's what everyone tells me.

❀ ❀ ❀

2 <u>I</u> play soccer with my cousin Tato and he says, "Marisol, your skin is brown like mine, but your hair is the color of carrots. You don't match!"

3 "Actually, my hair is the color of fire," <u>I</u> say and kick the ball over Tato's head and into the goal.

I think
Shes
going
to Math

4 **M**y brother says, "Marisol, those pants don't match that shirt! They clash."

5 But I love green polka dots and purple stripes. I think they go great together. Don't you?

clash Colors or patterns that clash look strange or ugly together.

6 I also love peanut butter and jelly burritos, and speaking Spanish, English, and sometimes both.

7 "Can I have a puppy? A furry, sweet *perrito*?" I ask my parents. "*Por favor*?"

8 "*Quizas,*" Mami says.

9 "Maybe," Dad says, smiling and winking.

winking   You are winking when you quickly blink one eye at someone because you share a joke or secret.

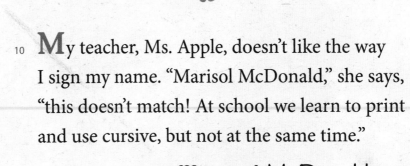

10 My teacher, Ms. Apple, doesn't like the way
I sign my name. "Marisol McDonald," she says,
"this doesn't match! At school we learn to print
and use cursive, but not at the same time."

11 But I like the way *Marisol* McDonald looks.

12 At recess, Ollie and Emma want to play pirates, and Noah wants to play soccer.

13 "How about soccer-playing pirates?" I suggest.

14 "No way!" they say, so I run off to play on the swings by myself.

15 After recess, we have art—my favorite subject. I think my drawings surprise my friends.

suggest If you suggest something, you give ideas or plans for someone to think about.

24

16 **A**t lunch, Ollie walks over to me and scrunches his nose.

17 "A peanut butter and jelly burrito?" he asks.

18 "I know, I know," I say, "it doesn't match. But it sure tastes good."

19 "Marisol, you couldn't match if you wanted to!" Ollie says.

20 "Oh yeah? I bet I can!"

scrunches If something scrunches up, it is squeezed or crushed into a different shape.

21   The next day I wake up and decide that today I, Marisol McDonald, will match.

22   It's a little hard to find clothes that are all the same color.

23   I play pirates with Ollie at recess, but it's not very fun. Why can't pirates play soccer, anyway?

24   I have a regular peanut butter and jelly sandwich at lunch and the bread tastes . . . mushy.

mushy Something that is mushy is soft and squishy.

parte de
el vuelo con
prefieres, tomar
erte un master de
de es posible
y gigantes para los aventureros.
de sumar una
monio con la expo
de una lona que dice
casar conmigo?".
Hotel Quinto Sol: Hidalgo 26
Purificación, San Juan Teoti
Estado de México / Lu a Do
horas / $1900 por persona
compartido; $2500 por pe
AEROSTÁTICO NACIONA
uelo de casi una hora por las
ñas de Tequisquiapan, con vista
la Peña de Bernal, los campos de
golf, las minas de ópalo y los pas
zales y sembradíos. Hay paquete
que incluyen una noche en La

myNotes

25 Even art class is a little bit boring.

26 "Marisol," Ms. Apple says, "What's wrong? This doesn't look like your usual work."

27 "I'm trying to match," I say with a frown.

28 "Why?" asks Ms. Apple.

29 I can't think of a single good reason.

usual The usual way to do something is the way that is done most often.

30 At the end of the day, Ms. Apple hands me a note. I open it and it says:

31 Marisol,

32 I want you to know that I like you just the way you are, because the Marisol McDonald that I know is a creative, unique, bilingual, Peruvian-Scottish-American, soccer-playing artist and simply marvelous!

33 —Ms. Jamiko Apple

34 I skip all the way home.

---

bilingual People who are bilingual can speak two languages.

35 **W**hen I wake up on Saturday I put on my pink shirt, my polka dot skirt, and my favorite hat—the one my *abuelita* brought me from Peru.

36 At breakfast I say, "My name is Marisol McDonald and I don't match because . . . I don't want to!"

37 "Bravo!" says Mami.

38 "Good for you," says Dad. "Now let's go to the pound and get a puppy!"

39 When we get to the pound, there are big dogs and little dogs. There are dogs with long noses and dogs with smushed faces. There are chocolate colored puppies and smoky gray puppies and puppies the color of caramel.

40 How will I ever choose?

41 Then I see him. He has one floppy ear and one pointy ear, one blue eye and one brown eye. He is beautiful!

CITY DOG POUND

42 I walk over and he leaps into my lap. I cuddle him and it sounds like he purrs.

43 "I think we found just the right dog for you, Marisol," Mami says.

44 My puppy is perfect. He's *mismatched* and simply marvelous, just like me. I think I'll name him . . .

Kitty!

✿ ✿ ✿

mismatched   Things that are mismatched do not fit or belong together.

Collaborative Discussion

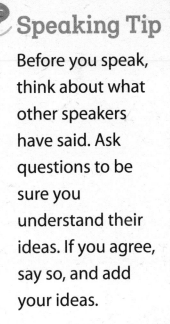

Look back at what you wrote on page 16. With a partner discuss your ideas about Marisol. Then work with a group to discuss the questions below. Refer to details in *Marisol McDonald Doesn't Match* to support your ideas. Take notes for your responses. When you speak, use your notes and think about ways to connect your ideas to what others have said.

1 Reread page 19. What do you learn about Marisol when she says her hair color is like fire rather than carrots?

> We learned that She dosent care What People think about her and shes confident.

2 Reread page 22. What does Ms. Apple think about the way Marisol writes her name?

> Ms. aPPlse thinks marisols name is mismated. She dosent like it

3 Review page 29. How does Marisol feel after reading Ms. Apple's note?

> Marisol feels delightful reading the note.

Listening Tip

Listen to the details and ideas each speaker discusses. What new information can you add?

Speaking Tip

Before you speak, think about what other speakers have said. Ask questions to be sure you understand their ideas. If you agree, say so, and add your ideas.

Write a Response

Respond to the Text You met an interesting and unique character in *Marisol McDonald Doesn't Match* by Monica Brown. Think about the events in the story. What did Marisol learn about herself? What makes her an interesting character to read about? Cite evidence from the text to support your response.

EVIDENCE

List ideas from *Marisol McDonald Doesn't Match* that show what Marisol learns and why. Then list details about why she is an interesting character.

* She learns that she dosnt have to be like others
* Marisol likes matching becase when she mathes she did not like in
* She dosnt have to be like the kids
* She learns thats she uivnide

becase she has spesial trats shes positive. Shes not bothered about what people think. Shes always mismatches

WRITE

Now write your response in a paragraph.

Make sure your response

- ☐ uses evidence from the story to answer the questions.
- ☐ explains what Marisol learns about herself.
- ☐ describes what makes Marisol an interesting character.
- ☐ is written in complete sentences.

Marisol that she enjoy being mismatced and dosent have to be like others. She learns that shes very unnivle also. Shes not bothered by others thoughts. Morisol is iteresting because shes confident, Positive, and brave. She also has a dog named Kitty. She has univle traits.

Notice & Note
Aha Moment

Prepare to Read

> **GENRE STUDY** **Realistic fiction** tells a story about characters and events that are like those in real life.

- The events in realistic fiction build on each other to keep the plot moving.
- Realistic fiction includes characters who act, think, and speak like real people.
- Realistic fiction may include sensory details and figurative language to appeal to the reader.
- Realistic fiction often includes dialogue to develop the story.

> **SET A PURPOSE** **Think about** the title and genre of this text. What kind of girl might Judy be? List some words below that could describe Judy.

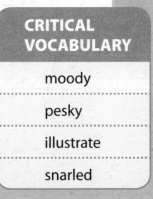

CRITICAL VOCABULARY

moody

pesky

illustrate

snarled

Meet the Author: Megan McDonald

JUDY MOODY

Mood Martian

by Megan McDonald

illustrated by Peter H. Reynolds

Who's Who

Not-Moody Judy

Stink

Rocky

Frank

Jessica

Mom

Dad

Amy

SHEEP SKATE

In a Mood

1 **S**he, Judy Moody, was in a mood. A sourball mood. A mad-face mood. All because school pictures had come home that day.

2 If Stink came into her room, he would ask to see her school picture. And if he asked to see her school picture, he would see that she had been wearing her I AM A GIRL, HEAR ME ROAR T-shirt. (The same one she wore today.) And if he saw her wearing her ROAR T-shirt in her school picture, he would also see that she looked like Sasquatch. With bird's-nest hair in her face and in her eyes.

3 Mom and Dad were going to freak. "Just once we'd like to have a nice school picture of our girl," Dad had said just this morning.

4 "Maybe this will be the year," Mom had said.

5 But third grade was no different.

moody If you are moody, your feelings change often and quickly.

6   Judy spread out her school pictures on the floor. She looked like:

A clown
(Kindergarten)

A one-eyed pirate
(Second grade)

Sasquatch
(Third grade)

7   If only Mom and Dad would forget about school pictures this year. Fat chance. Maybe Judy could pretend the dog ate them! Too bad the Moodys didn't have a dog. Only Mouse the cat. She could say that an evil school-picture bandit erased them from the master computer. Hardly.

8   To make things worse, Rocky had grabbed her Sasquatch picture in class and wouldn't give it back. Then he passed it to Frank, which made Judy yelp and jump up out of her seat instead of doing her math. That's when Mr. Todd said the *A* word.

9   *Antarctica.*

10   The desk in the back of the room where Judy had to go to chill out. For the third time that day! Never in the History of Judy had she been to Antarctica that many times in a row.

11   A donut-sized sicky spot sat in her stomach just remembering it.

12   That's why she, Judy Moody, was in a mood. A finger-knitting, don't-think-about-school-pictures, need-to-be-alone mood. As in *by herself.* As in no stinky little brother to bug and bother her like a pesky mosquito. *Bzzz!* Stink was always in her ear.

---

pesky   Something that is pesky is annoying.

13　　Judy's Number One Favorite Place to curl up with Mouse was on her top bunk, but Stink would for-sure find her there. She crawled over gobs of flip-flops and blobs of dirty clothes to her second favorite spot to be alone—the way-back of her closet. She popped a wad of Stink's yard-long bubble gum in her mouth.

14　　"Don't look at me like that, Mouse. What Stink doesn't know won't hurt him." She picked up a skein of gray-brown yarn and looped it around her thumb. Mouse batted the finger-knitting chain with her paw.

15　　Over. Under. Over. Under. Back. Loop-de-loop-de-loop. Judy tugged on the long chain of apple-green yarn that dangled from her left hand. Her fingers flew. She, Judy Moody, was the fastest finger knitter in Frog Neck Lake, Virginia. The fastest finger knitter in the east. Probably the fastest in the whole wide world!

16　　Finger knitting was the greatest—no knitting needles needed. She looped the yarn over her fingers, one, two, three, four, back over, under, through . . . just like Grandma Lou had taught her during the big blackout of Hurricane Elmer.

17　　Judy's closet was like a secret little room all to herself. It even had a window. A small, round window just like the kind they had on ships. Sailing ships. Pirate ships.

18　　*The ship sailed across the blue ocean, bobbing on the waves under a sky full of marshmallow clouds. Judy and Mouse rocked back and forth as the ship's hammock swung in the breeze. Until the ship hit a giant wave and . . .*

19　　*Mouse overboard!*

20　　*Judy tossed her chain of knitting to Mouse. She felt a tug on the line. It was—*

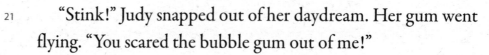

21   "Stink!" Judy snapped out of her daydream. Her gum went flying. "You scared the bubble gum out of me!"

22   "Where'd you get that gum?" asked Stink.

23   "Nowhere. It's ABC gum." She picked it up and popped it back in. "How'd you find me, anyway?"

24   "I followed the chain of yarn."

25   The long, colorful chain of finger knitting snaked across the bottom of her closet, climbed up and over piles of books and towers of toys, wound around Sock Mountain, and crept out the door.

26   "Well, bad idea. I'm in a mood."

27   "How was I supposed to know?"

28   "Clues one, two, and three: those doohickeys that hang on the doorknob?"

29   "Oh, I thought you were going to say school pictures."

30   "That, too."

31   "Somebody's in a mood."

32   "Bingo!"

33   "Can I help it if I don't go around reading doorknobs?"

34   Judy looked around and grabbed a fuzzy pillow. "See this pillow? This will be my mood pillow. It'll be our signal. If the pillow's sitting up, it means *I'm in a good mood. Come on in.* But if it's lying down—*Bad mood.* Go away. Much better than a doorknob doohickey."

35   "But what if the pillow was standing up and the window was open and a hurricane came and super-high winds blew down the pillow and knocked it on its side? Or what if a giant monster bigger than King Kong came and picked up our house and shook it like a toothpick and the pillow fell over?"

36   "Fine." Judy plucked a marker from her pencil box. She set the pillow in her lap. On one side, she drew a happy face for *good* mood. On the other side, she drew a frowny face for *bad* mood.

37   "This will be my mood pillow. Happy face means *Come on in.* Frowny face means *Go away.*" Judy leaned the pillow against the wall—frowny face out. "The pillow has spoken, Stink."

The Jessica Experiment

38   She, Judy Moody, had an idea. A not-bad mood idea. She was going to try to be in a good mood for one whole week.

39   Judy asked her friends, "Hey, guys. What puts you in a good mood?"

40   "When I do a really good magic trick, like the Fake Finger trick," said Rocky. He pulled his index finger, pretending to yank it off. "If everybody claps and is amazed, it puts me in a good mood."

41   "Uh-huh," Judy scribbled a Note to Self.

42   "I get in a good mood when I'm done with my homework," said Frank.

43   "Uh-huh, uh-huh." Judy looked at her notes.

44   Next it was Amy's turn. "Writing stories puts me in a good mood. I dream stuff up and make it into a book and illustrate it."

illustrate   If you illustrate a book, you draw pictures that go with the story.

45 Judy scribbled some more. She looked at her notes.

46 *1. Magic trick*

47 *2. Homework*

48 *3. Write a story*

49 "I can do this," said Judy.

50 "Do what?" asked Amy.

51 "Do what?" asked Rocky and Frank.

52 "Um . . . nothing. Never mind."

53 Judy ran home and took out her list. *Magic Trick*. She tried a magic card trick on Stink. But all she did was spill the deck of cards everywhere. *Homework*. Judy did not see how homework would put her in a good mood. She crossed it off the list. *Write story*. Judy tried to write a story.

54 This story could go on and on and on. What a lemonhead! Writing a story was so *not* putting her in a good mood. Who else could she get ideas from? Mom? Dad? Stink?

55 It had to be somebody smart and somebody who never got sent to Antarctica.

45

56   Wait just a ding-dong minute! What could be more perfect than to talk to Little Miss Perfect? Somebody who brushed her hair every day and followed all the rules and got good grades and had never even been *near* Antarctica.

57   Somebody who had a *happy* Magic 8 Ball.

58   Jessica A-plus Finch! Of course!

59   Judy could learn the facts about doing everything right all the time. Being perfect was sure to put her in a good mood. All she had to do was study her subject. Like a science experiment!

60   She grabbed her notebook and hopped on her bike and pedaled down the street and around the corner to Jessica Finch's house.

61   *Ding-dong!* Judy rang the bell. Jessica A-not-Aardwolf opened the door.

62   "Judy Moody? What are you doing here?"

63   She could not tell Jessica "Tell-All" Finch her secret. Then the whole world would know. "I, um, thought we could hang out," said Judy.

64   "But you never want to hang out."

65   "Never say never," said Judy, pushing past Jessica. "Can I come in?"

66   "You are in," said Jessica.

67   "Well, um, how about if I come up to your room?"

68   "Sure," said Jessica. "I was just going to start measuring things for Measure Up!, our new math unit."

69   "But that doesn't start till Thursday," said Judy.

70   "I like to get a head start," said Jessica.

71   Judy perched on the edge of the bed next to Jessica. She bounced up and down, testing out the jump factor.

72   "My mom doesn't like me to bounce on the bed," said Jessica.

73   "Check," said Judy. She scribbled *DO NOT BOUNCE ON BED* in her notebook. Judy stared sideways at Jessica. Her hair was brushed back into a very neat ponytail and she was wearing pink. Judy wrote *PUT HAIR IN PONYTAILS* and *WEAR PINK* in her notebook.

74   "Why are you staring at me?" asked Jessica. "It's rude."

75   "No reason," said Judy. She looked around. The bed was made and there were a hundred million fluffy pink pillows on it. Stuffed-animal pigs were lined up in a row on the dresser. So was a piggy-bank collection.

76   No books or clothes were on the floor. No arts-and-crafts supplies were on the floor. No gum wrappers were on the floor. A pink robot poster on the wall said OBEY. It was creepy, but Judy didn't say so.

77   "Your floor is very neat," said Judy. "I can see the rug."

78   "Thanks," said Jessica. "I like my room clean. It puts me in a good mood."

79   "Check." Judy wrote *CLEAN ROOM* in her notebook.

80   "Why are you writing stuff down?" asked Jessica.

81   "No reason," said Judy, sniffing the air. "I smell cupcakes. Do you smell cupcakes?"

82   Jessica cackled. "That's my lip gloss." She flipped open a teeny-tiny pink plastic cupcake. Inside was gooey lip stuff. Judy tried some. Yum, yum! Maybe cupcake lip gloss was another key to a good mood.

83   Judy wrote down *WEAR CUPCAKE LIP GLOSS.* "You like smiley faces, huh?" In Jessica's room, Judy saw a smiley-face pillow, pencil holder, and paper clips. She saw smiley-face sunglasses and slippers. Even a smiley-face mobile hung over Jessica's desk. She picked up Jessica's smiley-face Magic 8 Ball. "Can I try?"

84   Jessica nodded.

85   Judy had a burning question. But it was a secret. So she asked herself the question silently. *Will I be able to stay in a good mood for one whole week?*

86   She shook the Happy 8 Ball. *Nice outfit.* She asked the question and shook it again. *Your breath is so minty!* She tried again. *You smell great.*

87   "It keeps telling me that I smell great," said Judy.

88   "It's the lip gloss." Jessica nodded knowingly. "Want to do homework now?"

89   Judy wrote *DO HOMEWORK ON TIME* in her notebook.

90   She also got out her Positively Pink see-through ruler. She got out her Positively Pink tape measure. She even had a Positively Pink yardstick.

91   "Wow. You have a yardstick? I have a yardstick of bubble gum. It's this long." She stretched out her arms. "Well, it used to be. There's actually only two and three-quarters inches of gum left. But the box is a yard-long ruler—for real! And it has jokes and—"

92   "I wouldn't use it for homework if I were you," said Jessica.

93   Judy looked around for something to measure. "Do you have a cat? We could measure stuff like the cat's tail!" said Judy.

94   Jessica crinkled her forehead. "I was just going to measure the carpet." She started to stretch the tape measure across the rug. Bor-ing!

95   This being in a good mood was harder than it looked. Judy's fingers itched.

96   If only she were back in her closet with her finger knitting.

97   She stared at Jessica some more. "Do you ever miss the bus to school?" Judy asked.

98   Jessica wrinkled her forehead again. "Why would I do that?"

99   "I mean, are you ever late to school? Say you slept late. Or read your book under the covers when you should have been getting ready. Or didn't do your Spelling homework and decided to stay home sick."

100   "I always do my Spelling homework. I never fake sick. And I have a Walkie Clockie," said Jessica. She pulled an alarm clock with wheels from her nightstand. "It beeps like a robot and jumps off my nightstand when it's time to get up. I have to get out of bed to chase it around."

101   "Can I try?" asked Judy.

102   "Sure." Jessica set the clock to go off in one minute. They waited. They waited some more.

103   *Eep! Beep!* Walkie Clockie leaped to the floor. "*Out of bed, sleepyhead.*" It zoomed across the carpet. "*Up and at 'em, madam!*" It zoomed under the bed. *"Rise and shine, friend of mine!"* Judy chased it all around Jessica's room.

104   "Wow!" said Judy. "It walks. It talks. It rhymes. It chimes." She wrote down *GET WALKIE CLOCKIE SO I'M NEVER LATE* in her notebook. "That was fun. Let's do it again. This time—"

105   "It's not really a game," said Jessica. She put the clock back on her nightstand. "C'mon, let's do our homework."

106   Judy looked at her to-do list. She had a lot to do if she was going to stay out of Antarctica. She had a lot to learn about being in a good mood. "I can't," said Judy. "I have to—um—go finish my science experiment."

107   "Science experiment?" Jessica sat up straight. Her eyes got wide. "What science experiment? We don't have any—"

108   But Judy was already down the steps and halfway out the front door.

109   *Yippee skippy!*

Spaghetti Yeti

110   First things first. As soon as Judy got home, she pulled her hair back into two Jessica Finch ponytails. Then she cleaned up her room like a friend without an *R. F-I-E-N-D*, spelling word #23 on Mr. Todd's homework list. Definition: maniac. She huffed and puffed, picking up books and games and art supplies and stuffed animals. Yawn-o-rama. Mouse watched her every move. She huffed and puffed more putting away shirts and shorts and socks and pajamas. Bor-ing times two!

111   Mouse pounced on a sock. "Give it. It's not play time, Mouse. I wish."

112   She even tossed her finger knitting into the closet.

113   Jessica Finch was cuckoo-for-coconuts if she thought cleaning your room could put you in a good mood.

114   Next Judy did her this-week homework. Read, read, read. Spell, spell, spell. Multiply. Divide. Done!

115   Doing her homework on time did not put her in a good mood.

116   "Now what, Mouse?" Judy asked. She checked her notebook. Eureka! She, Judy Moody, had an idea.

117   Judy dug and dug like a badger to the way-back of her closet. She pulled out her last-year Christmas presents. Under the hand-knitted dancing mouse sweater

from Grandma Lou was a present from Nana and Gramps in California. It was not a way-cool Make-Your-Own Gum kit. It was not a way-cool Make-Your-Own Seashell Night-Light kit. It was a Make-Your-Own Lip Gloss kit! Cotton candy, chocolate, *cupcake!!* Double exclamation point!!

118   Last Christmas, Judy would not have been caught dead wearing smelly lip gloss. But that was before the Jessica experiment. She had to try it now—in the name of good moods.

119   Judy did not want to mess up her clean room, so she messed up the bathroom instead. Warm water, sticky hands, smelly flavor and . . . *voilà!* Cupcake lip gloss.

120   *Mww! Mww! Mww!* Judy looked in the mirror and smacked her lips. *Yum, yum.* She licked her lips. Oops. Now she needed more lip stuff. *Smack, smack, smack.* Lip-smacking good! Cupcake lip stuff *did* put her in a bit of a better mood. Who knew?

121   Judy went back to her room. *Sing a song of tuna fish!* Her finger-knitting chain snaked and snarled out the closet door, up, over, and around the doorknob across the dresser, and onto the floor, where Mouse was curled up sleeping on a heap of it.

snarled   If something is snarled, it is twisted and tangled.

122 Judy tugged an end out from under Mouse. "Who yarn bombed my clean room, Mouse?" she said. "Don't even try to say it was Stink."

123 At last, she had time for her new rave—finger knitting. She went to her closet to get some more yarn. But there was no more yarn. Not one ball. Not one skein. Not even a snippet. She was O-U-T *out*.

124 Judy ran downstairs. "Mom! Mom! Can we go to Bullseye? It's a yarn emergency!"

125 "Sorry, honey," said Mom. "All this yarn costs money. Let's wait and ask Grandma Lou for some yarn next time we see her."

126 "But . . . !" Judy was about to say it was so not fair. Judy was about to say she could not wait. Judy was about to stomp up the stairs. But that would mean she was in a mood. Not a good mood. A bad mood.

127 Judy dashed back upstairs. Her frowny-face mood pillow glared at her.

128 It was only GMD #1, Good Mood Day Number One. Judy had to be stomp-free for the rest of the week. This being in a good mood all the time sure was not as easy-peasy, mac-and-cheesy as it looked.

Collaborative Discussion

Look back at what you wrote on page 36. Discuss your ideas and list of words with a partner. Then work with a group to discuss the questions below. Refer to details and examples from *Judy Moody, Mood Martian* and take notes for your responses. Remember to listen carefully to what others say and to wait for your turn to speak.

1 Reread page 39. What can you tell about the reasons that Judy often goes to a place in the classroom called *Antarctica*?

> Judy goes to antartica to chill becase shes upset with other class mates.

2 Reread pages 39–40. Why does Judy like finger knitting?

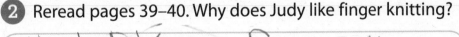

> Judy likes fingern kititing because it cames her down it keeps her focoused and she only needs fingers

3 Reread pages 46–47. What does Judy hope to learn when she visits Jessica? Why is it important for Judy to learn?

> Judy hopes to learn how to be in a good mood becouse she dosnt want to be in antartica

Write a Response

PROMPT

Respond to the Text In *Judy Moody, Mood Martian*, the author uses interesting details to tell about Judy. What details did you find most interesting? What questions would you ask Judy if you could meet her in real life? Cite evidence from the text to support your response.

EVIDENCE

List details from *Judy Moody, Mood Martian* that help make Judy interesting to readers.

Judy changes to a bad mood into a good
She likes finger knitting.
Judy ends up enjoying flavored lip gloss.
Judy has a brother named Stink.
She can change her by learning from Jecica.

WRITE

Now write your response in a paragraph.

Make sure your response

- [x] uses details from the story.
- [x] tells how the author made the characters interesting to readers.
- [x] includes questions you might ask Judy.
- [ ] is written in complete sentences.

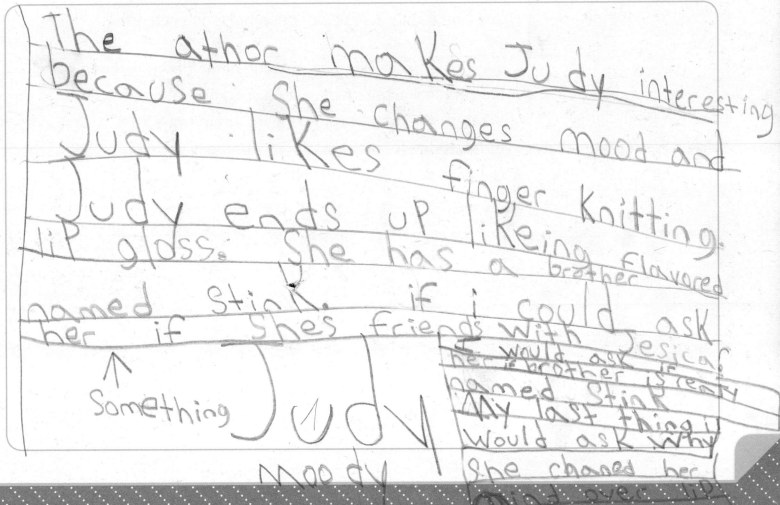

The athor makes Judy interesting because she changes mood and Judy likes finger knitting. Judy ends up likeing flavored lip gloss. She has a brother named Stink. if i could ask her if shes friends with Jesica. ↑ Something Judy Moody would ask her if brother is realy named Stink My last thing I would ask why she chaned her mind over lip gloss.

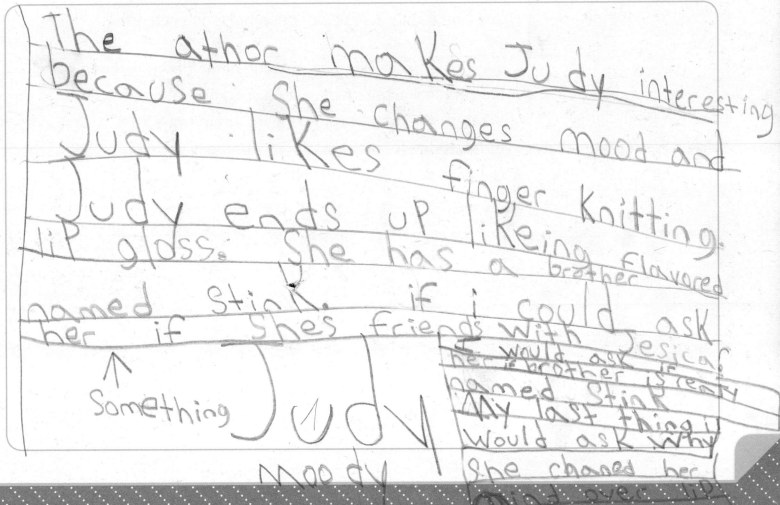

Prepare to Read

GENRE STUDY **Realistic fiction** tells a story about characters and events that are like those in real life.

- Realistic fiction includes characters who act, think, and speak like real people.
- Realistic fiction includes dialogue between characters to develop the story.
- The events in realistic fiction build on each other.

SET A PURPOSE **Think about** the genre of this text and look at the illustrations. What do you know about frogs? What do you think you could learn about frogs from Stink as he studies for his quiz? Write your ideas.

Tadpoles age ito frogs and there mothers lleave them.

CRITICAL VOCABULARY

annual

recited

protested

Meet the Illustrator:
Peter H. Reynolds

Stink
and the
Freaky
Frog Freakout

by Megan McDonald

illustrated by Peter H. Reynolds

* * *

1   Judy Moody's younger brother, Stink, has been finding frogs all over the place—at the pool, in his boot, even in the bathtub! When Stink and his friends visit a nature center to learn about frogs, they find out about the First Annual Frog Neck Lake Frog Count. Before he can participate in the late-night adventure, though, Stink has to study different frogs and the sounds they make . . . and pass a quiz!

* * *

annual   An annual event happens once each year.

2   *Pree-eep! Craw-awk! Sque-enk!*

3   Stink listened to frog calls on the computer. He listened to frog sounds that he taped with his own tape recorder (by sticking it out the window at night!). Stink listened to frog calls on the way to school Monday morning and in the car on the way to swim lessons.

4   *Pre-eep! Craw-awk! Sque-enk!* At swim practice, he tried some out on his friends.

5   "You sound like a duck," said Webster.

6   "You sound like a squeak toy," said Sophie.

7   "You sound like a sick banjo," said Riley.

8   "Thanks!" said Stink. "See, spring peepers sound like squeak toys. And wood frogs sound like ducks quacking."

9   "You're quacked," said Webster. Sophie and Riley cracked up.

10   "You guys sound like Southern leopard frogs. A leopard frog sounds like a person laughing. No lie."

11   "Yeah, but nothing sounds like a sick banjo," said Riley.

12   "Nothing except for the Northern green frog. It sounds like a loose banjo string. You know, like a rubber-band twang."

13   "You sure are freaky for frogs," said Riley.

14   "Thanks!" said Stink.

15   "You should marry a frog, you like them so much."

16   "Hardee-har-har," said Stink.

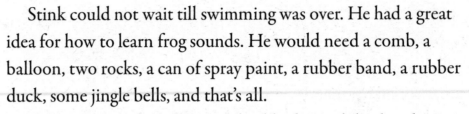

* * *

17 Stink could not wait till swimming was over. He had a great idea for how to learn frog sounds. He would need a comb, a balloon, two rocks, a can of spray paint, a rubber band, a rubber duck, some jingle bells, and that's all.

18 Stink blew up the balloon and rubbed it with his hand. He clicked rocks together. He twanged a rubber band.

19 Judy poked her head into Stink's room. Mouse, the family cat, squeezed past her.

20 "Stink, I'm trying to study my times tables and I can't hear myself—" She stopped when she saw the pile of junk on Stink's floor.

21   "What? I'm using this stuff to make frog sounds. Here.
I'll show you." Stink rubbed his finger along the teeth of a
comb. "This sounds like a chorus frog." Stink shook the can
of spray paint.

22   "And this sounds like a Northern cricket frog."

23   Mouse darted under the bed.

24   "And this—*AARGH!*—sounds like Mom when she sees the
mess in your room," said Judy.

25   "Hardee-har-har," chuckled Stink. "You're *croaking* me up!"

26   "Can you please shut your door so I don't have to hear
Froggle Rock all day?"

27   Stink squeaked his rubber duck down the stairs. He snored up a storm while he made a snack. He shook the can of paint, clicked the stones, and jingled the bells. "Wood frog, pickerel frog, cricket frog," he recited.

28   "Stink, keep it down, please," said Dad, poking his head around the corner. "I'm on the phone."

29   "No spray-painting in the house," said Mom. "Take that outside."

30   "I'm not painting," said Stink. "Doesn't anybody around here know a Northern cricket frog when they hear one?"

31   Mom crinkled her forehead.

32   "It's homework," said Stink. "I have to take a test."

33   "A *frog* test," said Judy, coming into the kitchen.

34   "I have to learn frog calls," said Stink. "For the First Annual Frog Neck Lake Frog Count on Friday."

35   "Riigggght," said Mom.

36   "It's a real thing. The test is on the computer," Stink told her. "You click on a frog and it makes a sound. Then you guess which frog is making that sound."

37   "Multiple choice?" said Judy. "Easy peasy," she teased.

38   "I have a multiple choice for you," said Mom. "You can go back upstairs and a) finish your homework, b) finish your homework, c) finish your homework, or d) all of the above."

---

recited   If you recited something, you said it aloud after you had learned it.

39　　　"But—" Stink protested.

40　　　"It's your choice," Mom said.

41　　　Stink trudged back up the stairs, with Judy close behind.

42　　　"And don't forget your NON-frog homework, too," Mom called.

　　　　　✷　★　✷

43　　　In Stink's room, Mouse curled up on his backpack. "How am I gonna learn all these frog calls by Tuesday?" Stink asked Judy. He held out his notebook for her to see. "You can't go on the frog count unless you pass the quiz."

44　　　"I'll help you," said Judy. "But let's make it a game. Instead of Rock, Paper, Scissors, we'll call it … Rock, Balloon, Squeak Toy."

45　　　"How do we play?"

46　　　"Close your eyes. I'll make a sound. You guess which frog it is. But we have to keep it down because Mom won't like us doing *frog* homework first."

47　　　"Okay, c'mon," said Stink. He squeezed his eyes shut. Judy rubbed the balloon. She twanged the rubber band. She clicked the stones.

protested　If you protested, you said why you did not agree with a statement or an idea.

48   "Mrrow!" Mouse pawed at the stones.

49   "Chorus frog. Wood frog. Cricket frog," Stink guessed.

50   Judy checked Stink's notebook. "Sorry. Leopard frog. Green frog. Cricket frog."

51   Stink hung his head.

52   "Hey, you got one right. Cricket frog. C'mon, Stink. Just get super-duper quiet. And really listen. Okay. Ready?"

53   "Ready, Freddy," said Stink.

54   Judy rubbed, clicked, squeaked, and twanged.

55   "Balloon, stones, squeak toy, rubber band," Stink said. "That's leopard frog, cricket frog, spring peeper, green frog."

56   "Bingo!" said Judy. She laughed, chuckled, whistled, peeped, snored, squeaked, jingled, and croaked until Stink knew pickerel frog from peeper, chorus frog from cricket.

57 "Yikes," said Judy, putting a *shh* finger to her lips. "I bet they can hear us all the way at the end of Croaker Road."

58 "Do you think they call our street Croaker Road because of all the frogs?"

59 "Because of animal frogs, Stink, not human boy frogs."

60 "Ribbet!" Stink croaked.

61 "Okay, close your eyes. I bet I can stump you. Ready?" Judy made a *zzzzz* sound.

62 "Bullfrog. No. Wood frog. No. Bullfrog." He opened his eyes.

63 "Zipper frog," said Judy. "That was just me zipping the zipper on your backpack."

64 "No fair," said Stink. "There's no such thing as a zipper frog."

65   "Mrrr-ow!" Mouse pounced on the jingle bells.

66   "Jingle frog!" Stink and Judy said at the same time. They cracked themselves up.

67   "We gotta finish our NOT-frog homework, Stink. Besides, you're like the Frog King now. No, you're like President of the Frogs. Now you just have to practice on real frogs."

68   "Sque-enk!" said Stink.

✶ ✶ ✶

69   On Tuesday, Stink Moody, Frog Genius, passed his test with flying colors. Frog test, that is.

70   Stink could not wait for Frog Friday.

Collaborative Discussion

Look back at what you wrote on page 58. Discuss your responses with a partner. Work with a group to discuss the questions below. Refer to details from the text and take notes.

1 Reread pages 60–61. How would you describe Stink's interest in frogs? Why?

> StinKs interested becaus

Listening Tip

Listen closely to other speakers. Think about how you can connect your ideas to theirs.

2 Reread pages 62–65. What are some of the sound effects Stink makes with different household objects? What does that tell you about Stink?

Speaking Tip

Be sure that all of your comments are about the topic your group is discussing.

3 What does the way Judy helps Stink with his homework tell you about Judy's personality?

Write a Response

PROMPT ....

Respond to the Text In *Stink and the Freaky Frog Freakout*, you learned about Judy Moody's younger brother, Stink. How would you describe Stink? What details does the author use to make Stink an interesting character to readers? Cite evidence from the text to support your response.

EVIDENCE ....

Write about how you would describe Stink. Then list details about Stink that make him an interesting character.

WRITE

Now write your response in a paragraph.

Make sure your response

- ☐ answers the questions.

- ☐ describes Judy's brother, Stink.

- ☐ lists details about Stink that make him an interesting character.

- ☐ uses details and examples from the text.

- ☐ is written in complete sentences.

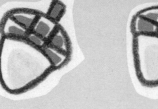

The Sientist
were venturing
for dino fosiles.
Gaby was
Per dict ble
for the whole
week.
MY friend
got into an
emergency

Prepare to Read

GENRE STUDY **Fantasies** are imaginative stories with characters and events that are not real. Some fantasies include elements of adventure or mystery.

- Authors of fantasy tell the story through the plot, including a conflict and its resolution.
- Some fantasies include illustrations that may give details about the plot, setting, and characters.
- Fantasies may include animals that act like people.
- Some fantasies include a theme.

SET A PURPOSE **Think about** the title and genre of this text. Why do you think the title is *Scaredy Squirrel*? What might make Squirrel feel scared? Write your ideas below.

He might be
stalked. He might
be scared of a
sectain animal.

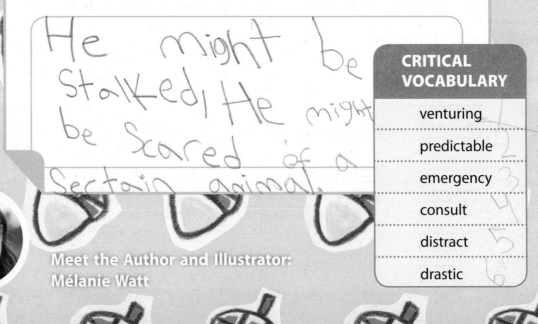

CRITICAL VOCABULARY

venturing

predictable

emergency

consult

distract

drastic

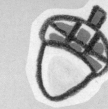

Meet the Author and Illustrator:
Mélanie Watt

Mélanie Watt

Scaredy Squirrel

Scaredy Squirrel never leaves his nut tree.

2 **He'd rather stay in his safe and familiar tree than risk venturing out into the unknown. The unknown can be a scary place for a squirrel.**

the unknown

venturing If you are venturing somewhere, you are going somewhere that is unfamiliar and may be unsafe.

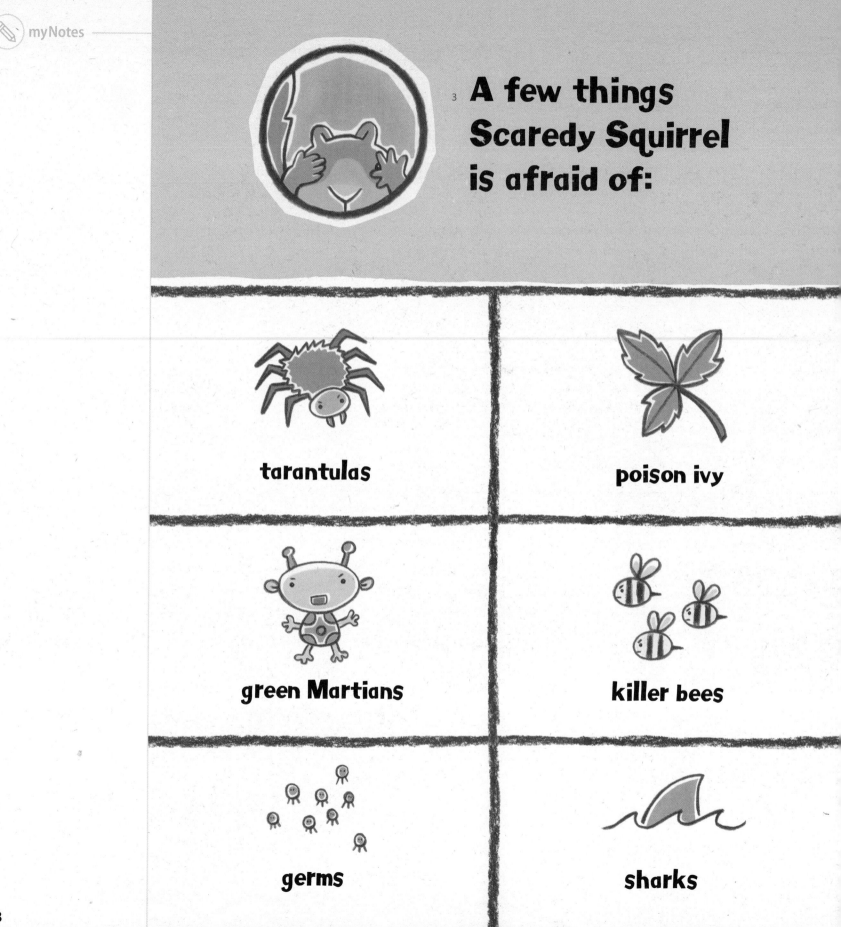

A few things Scaredy Squirrel is afraid of:

tarantulas

poison ivy

green Martians

killer bees

germs

sharks

4 **So he's perfectly happy
to stay right where he is.**

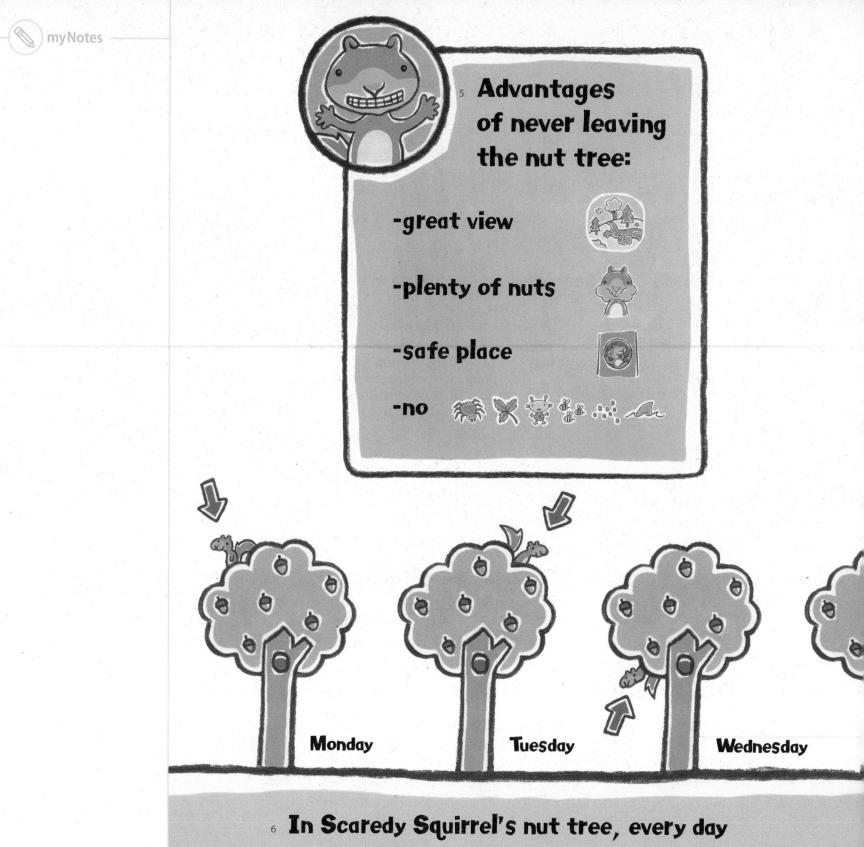

5 **Advantages of never leaving the nut tree:**

-great view

-plenty of nuts

-safe place

-no 🦀 🍃 🐛 🐝 ✨ 🌊

Monday   **Tuesday**   **Wednesday**

6 **In Scaredy Squirrel's nut tree, every day is the same.**

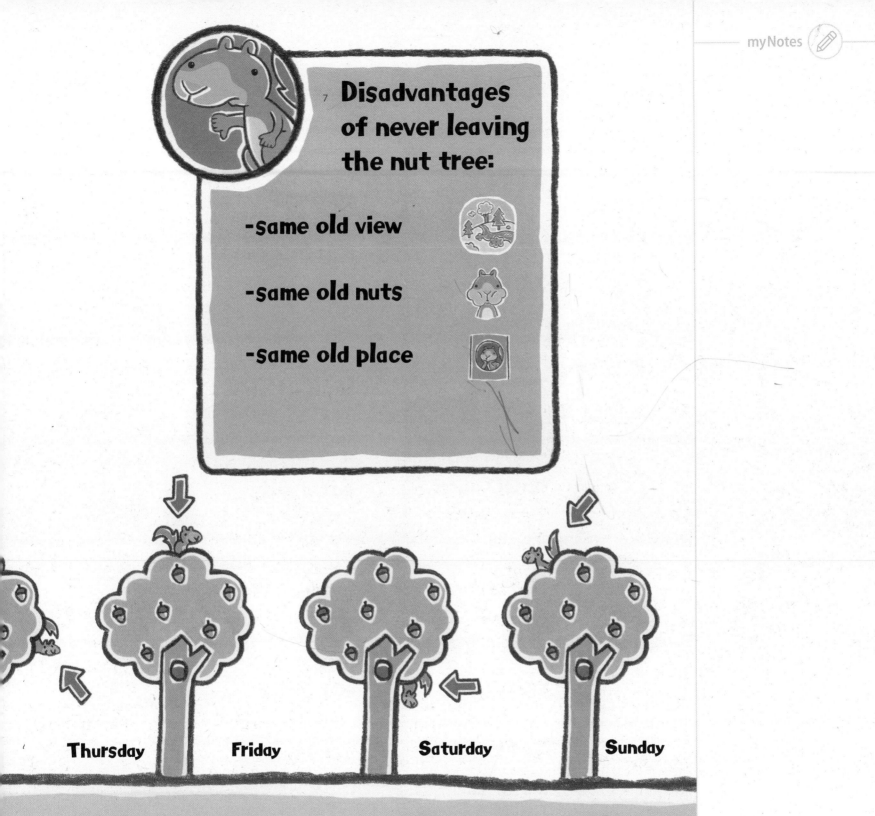

7 **Disadvantages of never leaving the nut tree:**

- same old view

- same old nuts

- same old place

Thursday   Friday   Saturday   Sunday

8 **Everything is predictable. All is under control.**

predictable   If something is predictable, it is just as you expect, with no surprises.

Scaredy Squirrel's daily routine:

6:45 a.m.	wake up	
7:00 a.m.	eat a nut	
7:15 a.m.	look at view	
12:00 noon	eat a nut	
12:30 p.m.	look at view	
5:00 p.m.	eat a nut	
5:31 p.m.	look at view	
8:00 p.m.	go to sleep	

10 **BUT** let's say, just for example, that something unexpected **DID** happen ...

11 **You can rest assured that this squirrel is prepared.**

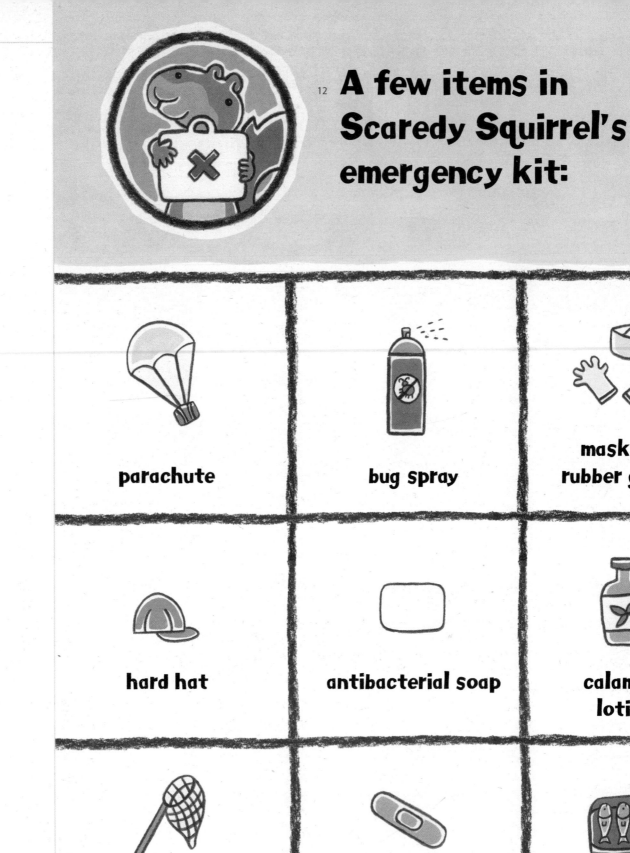

12 **A few items in Scaredy Squirrel's emergency kit:**

parachute

bug spray

mask and rubber gloves

hard hat

antibacterial soap

calamine lotion

net

bandage

sardines

13 **What to do in case of an emergency according to Scaredy Squirrel:**

Dramatization

14 **Step 1: Panic**

Step 2: Run

Step 3: Get kit

Step 4: Put on kit

Step 5: Consult Exit Plan

Step 6: Exit tree (if there is absolutely, definitely, truly no other option)

emergency   An emergency is an unexpected situation that requires help or quick action to make it better.

consult   If you consult something, you look at it to find information.

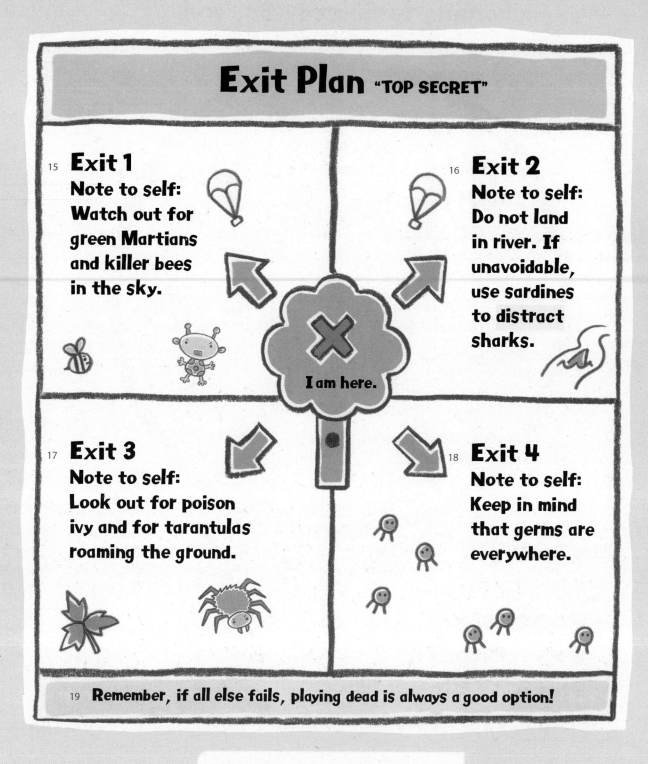

Exit Plan "TOP SECRET"

Exit 1
15 Note to self: Watch out for green Martians and killer bees in the sky.

Exit 2
16 Note to self: Do not land in river. If unavoidable, use sardines to distract sharks.

I am here.

Exit 3
17 Note to self: Look out for poison ivy and for tarantulas roaming the ground.

Exit 4
18 Note to self: Keep in mind that germs are everywhere.

19 Remember, if all else fails, playing dead is always a good option!

distract If you distract someone, you focus their attention away from something.

20 **With his emergency kit in hand, Scaredy Squirrel watches. Day after day he watches, until one day ...**

21 **Thursday
9:37 a.m.**

A killer bee appears!

22

23 **Scaredy Squirrel jumps in panic, knocking his emergency kit out of the tree.**

24 **This was NOT part of the Plan.**

25 **Scaredy Squirrel jumps to catch his kit.**
He quickly regrets this idea.
The parachute is in the kit.

26 **But something incredible happens ...**

27 **He starts to glide.**

28 **Scaredy Squirrel is no ordinary squirrel.**

29 **He's a FLYING squirrel!**

30 **Scaredy Squirrel forgets all about the killer bee, not to mention the tarantulas, poison ivy, green Martians, germs and sharks.**

31 **He feels overjoyed!**

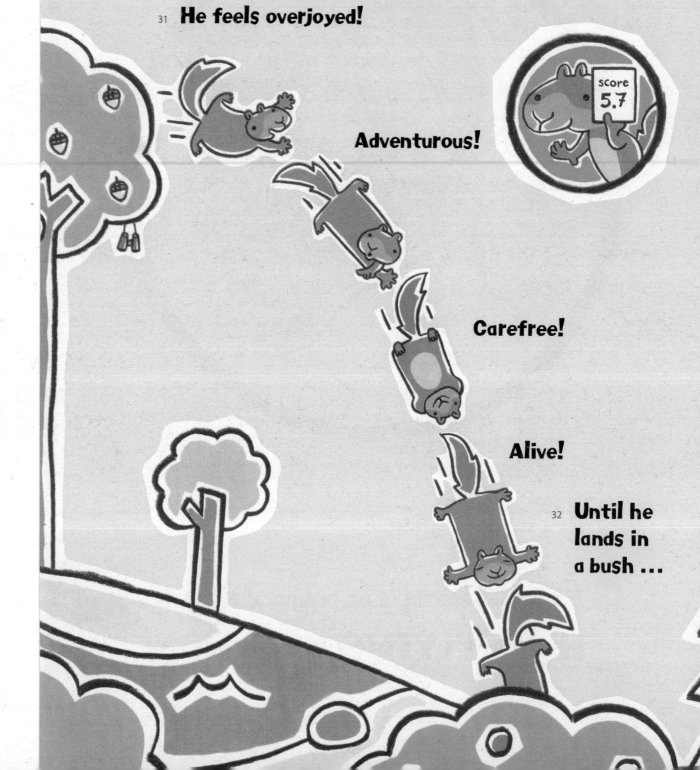

score
5.7

Adventurous!

Carefree!

Alive!

32 **Until he lands in a bush ...**

37 **Finally Scaredy Squirrel realizes that nothing horrible is happening in the unknown today. So he returns to his nut tree.**

38 **All this excitement has inspired Scaredy Squirrel to make drastic changes to his life ...**

drastic If you make a drastic change, you do something very different from what you have always done.

39 Scaredy Squirrel's new-and-improved daily routine:

6:45 a.m.	wake up	
7:00 a.m.	eat a nut	
7:15 a.m.	look at view	
9:37 a.m.	jump into the unknown	
9:45 a.m.	play dead	
11:45 a.m.	return home	
12:00 noon	eat a nut	
12:30 p.m.	look at view	
5:00 p.m.	eat a nut	
5:31 p.m.	look at view	
8:00 p.m.	go to sleep	

40 **P.S.** As for the emergency kit, Scaredy Squirrel is in no hurry to pick it up just yet.

THE
END

poison
ivy

Collaborative Discussion

Look back at what you wrote on page 74. Discuss your ideas with a partner. Work with a group to discuss the questions below. Refer to details from *Scaredy Squirrel*. Take notes for your responses. Remember to pay close attention to the other people in your group as you discuss.

1. Review page 78. Which of the things Scaredy Squirrel is afraid of might really hurt him? Which seem silly or surprising? Why?

> The toratila could bite
> Seardy Squirrl. Its funny how
> hes scared of sharks even
> though hes by a river.

2. Review pages 84–86. What do you learn about Scaredy Squirrel from his emergency kit and his exit plan?

> I learned that hes
> prepared for any crazy
> event thats comeing at him.
> kind of

3. How is Scaredy Squirrel different at the end of the story?

> Scaredy Sicle has very
> big brayecy.

Listening Tip

Listen carefully. Show your interest by turning or looking toward each speaker.

Speaking Tip

As you talk, notice the faces of the other group members. If someone looks confused, invite that person to ask you a question.

Mélanie Watt
Scaredy Squirrel

Write a Response

PROMPT

Respond to the Text In *Scaredy Squirrel*, you read about Scaredy Squirrel's daily routine. How would you describe Scaredy Squirrel? How did his beliefs and attitudes change from the beginning of the story to the end? Cite evidence from the text to support your response.

EVIDENCE

List details from *Scaredy Squirrel* that describe Scaredy and show how his beliefs and attitudes change.

WRITE

Now write your response in a paragraph.

Make sure your response

☐ answers the questions.
☐ uses details from the story.
☐ describes Scaredy Squirrel and how his beliefs and attitudes change.
☐ is written in complete sentences.

? Essential Question

What makes a character interesting?

Write an Expository Essay

PROMPT Think about how the authors in this module make their characters interesting. What character traits, words, and behaviors stand out? What do the illustrations show? Write an expository essay that explains how an author makes characters interesting to readers. Use evidence from the module selections to support your ideas.

✓ Make sure your expository essay
☐ introduces your topic.
☐ describes the characters' traits, words, and behaviors.
☐ explains how the authors make their characters interesting.
☐ uses text evidence and examples from the selections.
☐ provides a conclusion.

.... Map your ideas.

Think about the characters you read about in this module. What makes each character someone to remember? How did the authors make those characters interesting to readers? Use the map below to plan your writing.

Characters	Interesting Details

DRAFT ·· Write your expository essay.

Use the information you wrote on page 101 to draft your expository essay.
Write a beginning paragraph that introduces your topic.

Write a middle paragraph that tells how the authors make their characters
interesting to readers. Use text evidence and transitions when explaining
your ideas about the different characters.

Write a conclusion that summarizes your ideas.

The revising and editing steps give you a chance to look carefully at your writing and make changes. Work with a partner to determine whether you have explained your ideas clearly. Use the questions below to help you.

✓ PURPOSE/ FOCUS	ORGANIZATION	EVIDENCE/ SUPPORT	ELABORATION	CONVENTIONS
☐ Do I answer the questions? ☐ Do I explain why each character is interesting?	☐ Do I have a clear introduction to my topic? ☐ Does my conclusion summarize my topic?	☐ Have I included text evidence about each character?	☐ Have I explained my ideas clearly? ☐ Have I used transitions to connect my ideas?	☐ Have I spelled all words correctly? ☐ Have I used correct punctuation? ☐ Have I used capitalization correctly?

PUBLISH ···················· Create a finished copy.

Make a final copy of your expository essay. Use your cursive writing skills.

Use Your Words

"The limits of my language means the limits of my world."
— Ludwig Wittgenstein

Essential Question

How do people use words to express themselves?

Get Curious Video

Stories

Types of Words Used in . . .

Poems

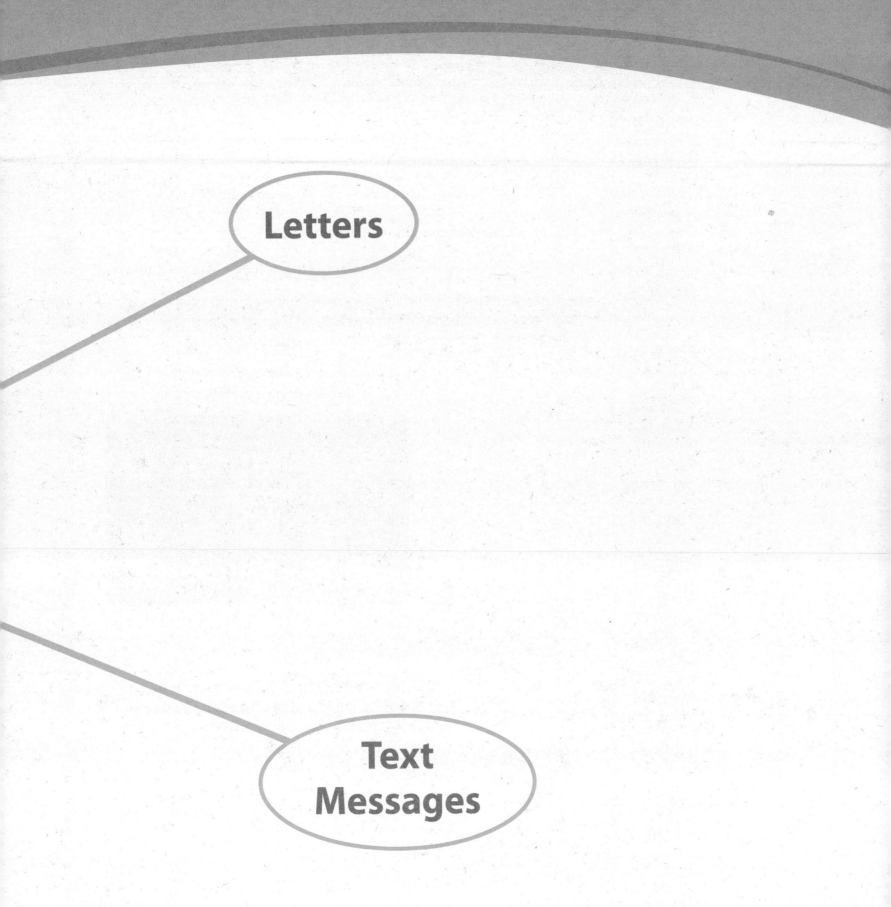

Letters

Text
Messages

Short Read

A LOL Story

Clara   **Martin**

1 Hey Martin, r u busy?

2 Hey Clara! Nope. What's up?

3 I'm reading the assignment for tomorrow.

4 I'm reading it 2, but I'm confused. Who is Zaron?

5 He's Abetha's pet, silly! In the beginning of the story, it says that he's her pet dragon. We need to read the selection and write an idea for another story with an unusual pet.

6 Right! Speaking of pets, check out this pic of my cat, Raymond.

7 LOL! 😎

8 So cute!! How'd you get him into space? 🚀

9 It's an app my mom downloaded, and I can use it to make any pet (or person) into an astronaut, a cowboy, or a football player!!!

10 FUN!!! Back to our homework . . . I can't think of a fun adventure. I'm not feeling very creative.

11 So you texted your BFF to brainstorm!

12 No, I texted YOU!

13 JK LOL

14 Anyway, the book is a fantasy, but I prefer realistic stories. I like it when authors are able to convey realistic plots and characters. No one has pet dragons IRL!

15 They have pet cats in spacesuits! BRB. Mom is calling me.

16 K.

17 Back. Raymond jumped on top of the kitchen cabinet, and I had to get him down with a liver treat. Liver! Ick!! 😖

18 LOL! That emoji really does express what u think of liver treats! How'd he get way up there, anyway??

19 I think he has secret wings because he always gets up to the highest spot in the room.

20 LOL! He's a high-flying kitten! 😸 🚀

21 HEY!!!!!!!!!!

22 Wait a minute!!!!!

23 NO WAY!

24 Yes, way! Here's an idea for a story: THE ADVENTURES OF SPACE KITTEN!

25 PURRRFECT!! It could be a chronicle of a cat who jumps so high that she launches into space!

26 Yes!

27 And she lands on Planet Mouse to look for adventure!

28 ROFL! 👍 🌍

29 Martin, u totally r my BFF!! TTYL, and THX a million! 😎 😊

30 Wait! Now what about an idea for MY story??!! 😳

Notice & Note
Aha Moment

Prepare to Read

GENRE STUDY **Realistic fiction** tells a story about characters and events that are like those in real life. **Letters** are written messages from one person to another.

- Realistic fiction includes characters who act like real people living in a time and place that seem real.

- Realistic fiction can be told through the eyes of a character or characters.

- Letters usually begin with a greeting and end with a closing.

SET A PURPOSE **Think about** the title and genres of this text. Look at the illustrations, too. What do you think this story is about? Write your ideas below.

1 People will send letters to each other.

Build Background: Immigration

CRITICAL VOCABULARY

video

hydrant

block

costumes

march

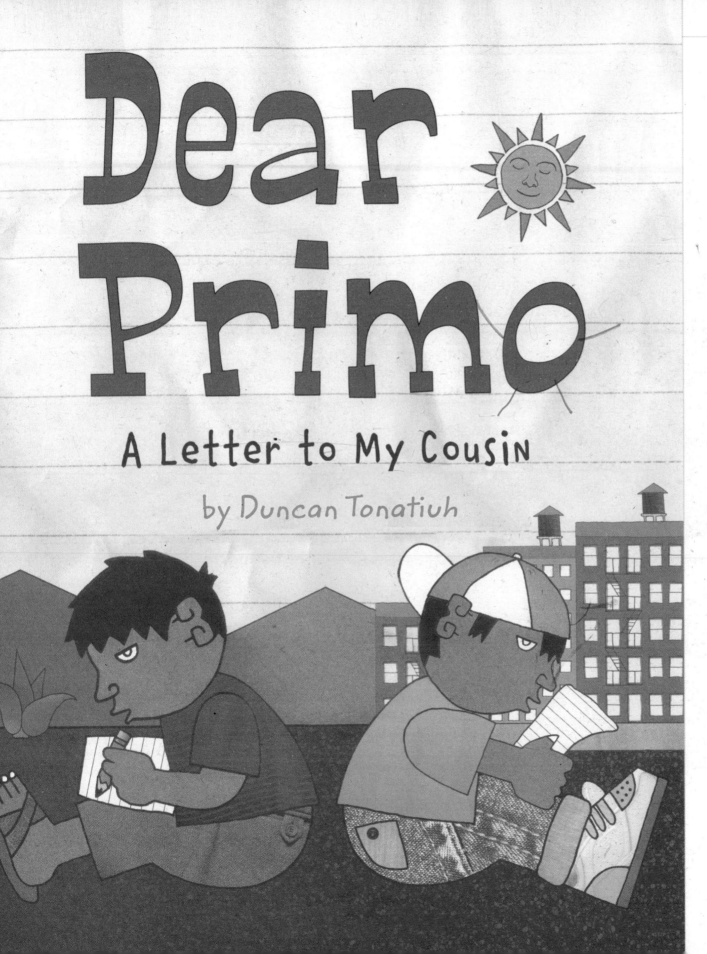

Dear Primo

A Letter to My Cousin

by Duncan Tonatiuh

1   Score! I just got a letter from
my *primo*, my cousin, Carlitos.
I live in America, but he lives in
Mexico, where my family is from.
Maybe someday we'll meet!

maíz

burro

gallo

pollos

2 Dear Primo Charlie,

3 How are you? Do you wonder like me
what life is like far away? I live on a farm
surrounded by mountains and trees. My
family grows many things, such as *maíz*.

4 We have a *burro*, *pollos*, and a *gallo*.
Every morning the *gallo* crows and crows.

5 **Dear Primo Carlitos,**

6 **I live in a city. From my window I can see a bridge and cars zooming by. I can see skyscrapers, too.**

7 **Skyscrapers are buildings so tall they tickle the clouds. At night all the lights from the city look like the stars from the sky.**

8 Every morning I ride my *bicicleta* to school.

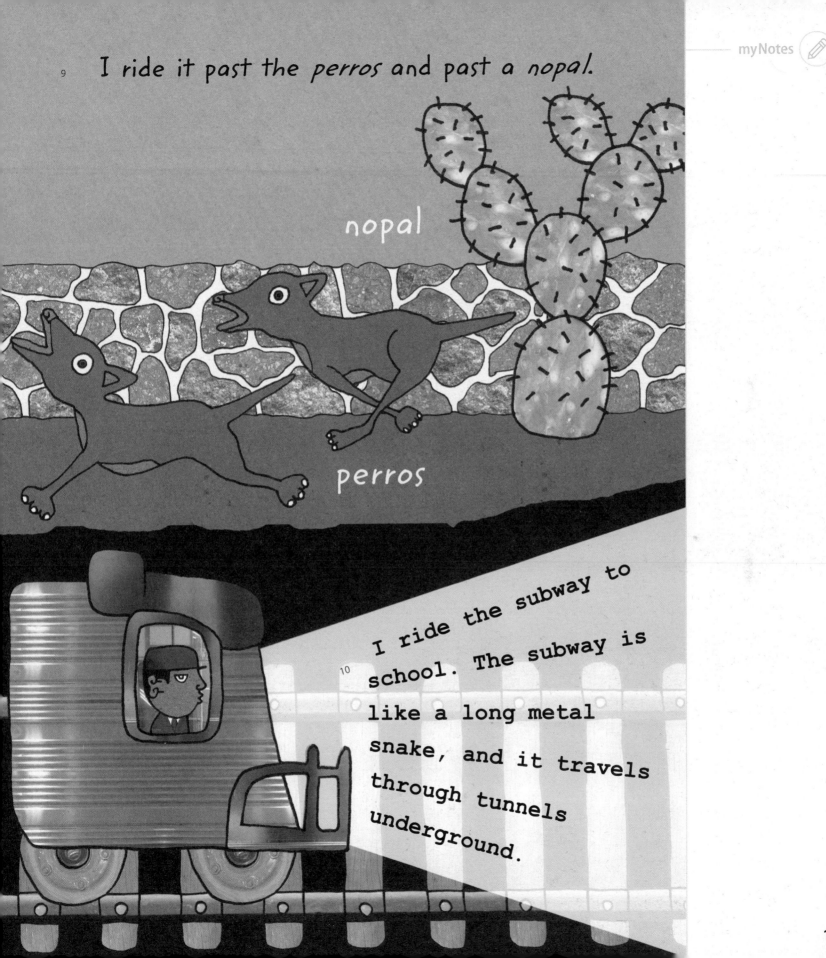

9 I ride it past the *perros* and past a *nopal*.

nopal

perros

10 I ride the subway to school. The subway is like a long metal snake, and it travels through tunnels underground.

11   At recess time I play *fútbol.* My friend passes me the ball, I kick it with my foot, and if I score, I yell...*gol!*

...*gol!*

12   I play basketball. My friend dribbles the ball and passes it to me. I jump and shoot.

The ball goes *swoosh*! Nothing but net.

13 When I come home from school, I help my mom cook. My favorite meal is quesadillas. I make them with cheese and tortillas.

quesadillas

tortillas

14 In America we have lots of different foods. My favorite is pizza. I like getting a slice on my way home from school.

15 After I finish my homework, my mom lets me go outside and play. In Mexico we have many games, like *trompos* and *canicas*.

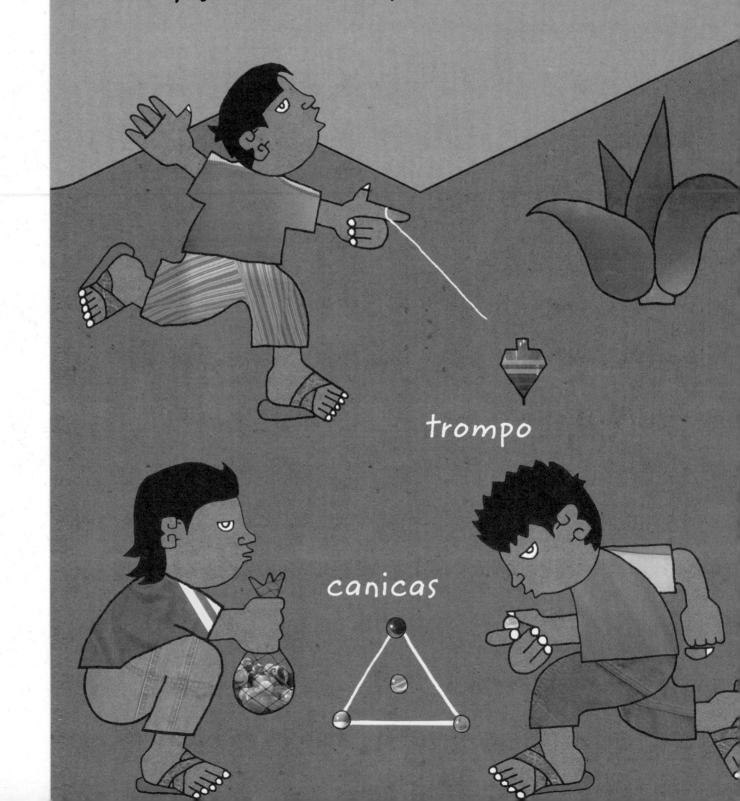

trompo

canicas

16 My favorite game is *papalotes*. My friends and I run and run, and with a little wind we fly the *papalote* high up.

papalote

17 When I finish my homework, I play games with my friends from the building. We play by the stoop . . .

18   . . . and in each other's apartments, too. I like going over to my friend's home to play video games.

> **video** The word video describes a recording of movements and actions that you can see on a television or computer screen.

río

19 In the afternoon it often gets hot. To cool off I jump in a small *río* that is nearby.

20   In the summer the city gets hot, too. I like getting splashed by the fire **hydrant** when the firefighters open it up and close off the **block**.

hydrant   A hydrant is an outdoor pipe firefighters use to get water to put out fires.

block   A block is a section of a community with streets on all of its sides.

On the weekend I go with my parents to the *mercado*, an open-air market in the town nearby. We sell *maíz* and *tunas*, a prickly fruit that we grow. We also buy the food and other things we need.

maíz

tunas

22   On the weekend I go with my mom to the supermarket. She brings a list—milk, toothpaste, soap—and I check off the items as we put them in our cart.

23 In the town from time to time they have *fiestas* that last two or three days. At night there are *cohetes* that light up the sky and *mariachis* that play and play.

cohetes

mariachis

24 In my city sometimes we have parades. People in **costumes** and uniforms **march** down the street, and everyone gathers around to watch.

costumes Costumes are special clothes that people may wear to pretend that they are from another time or place.

march When people march, they walk with even steps, often in a group.

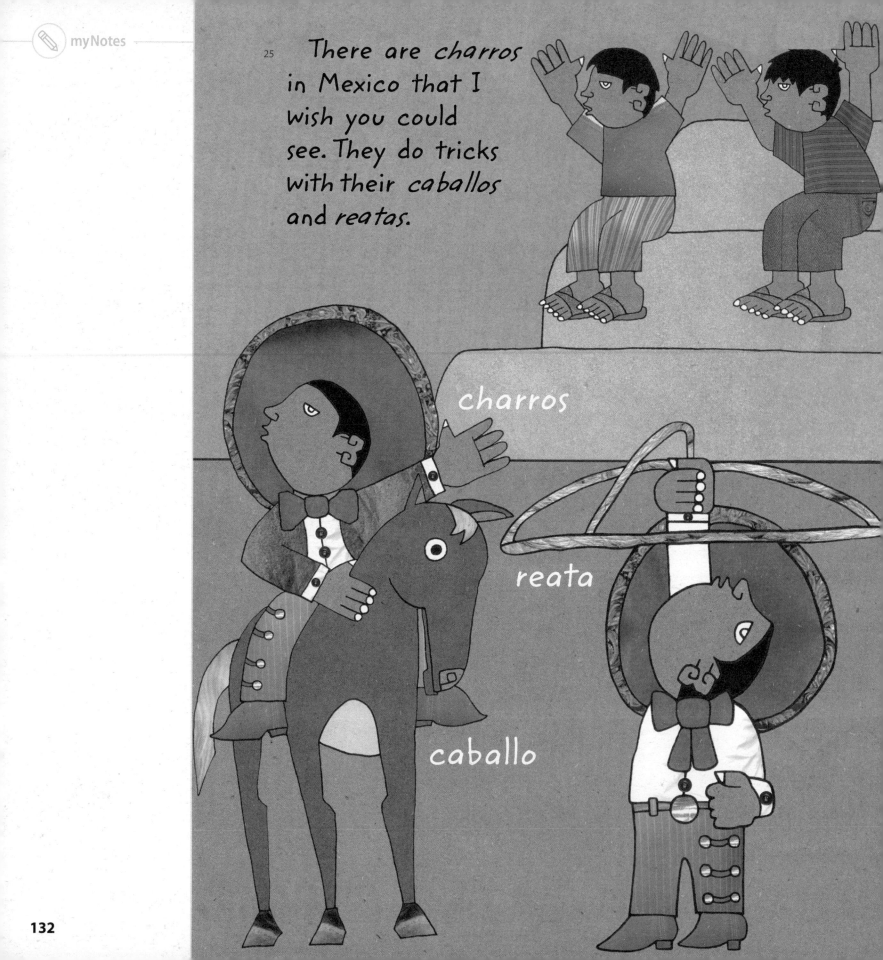

25 There are *charros* in Mexico that I wish you could see. They do tricks with their *caballos* and *reatas*.

charros

reata

caballo

On the streets here you can see break-dancers who do flips and spin on their heads.

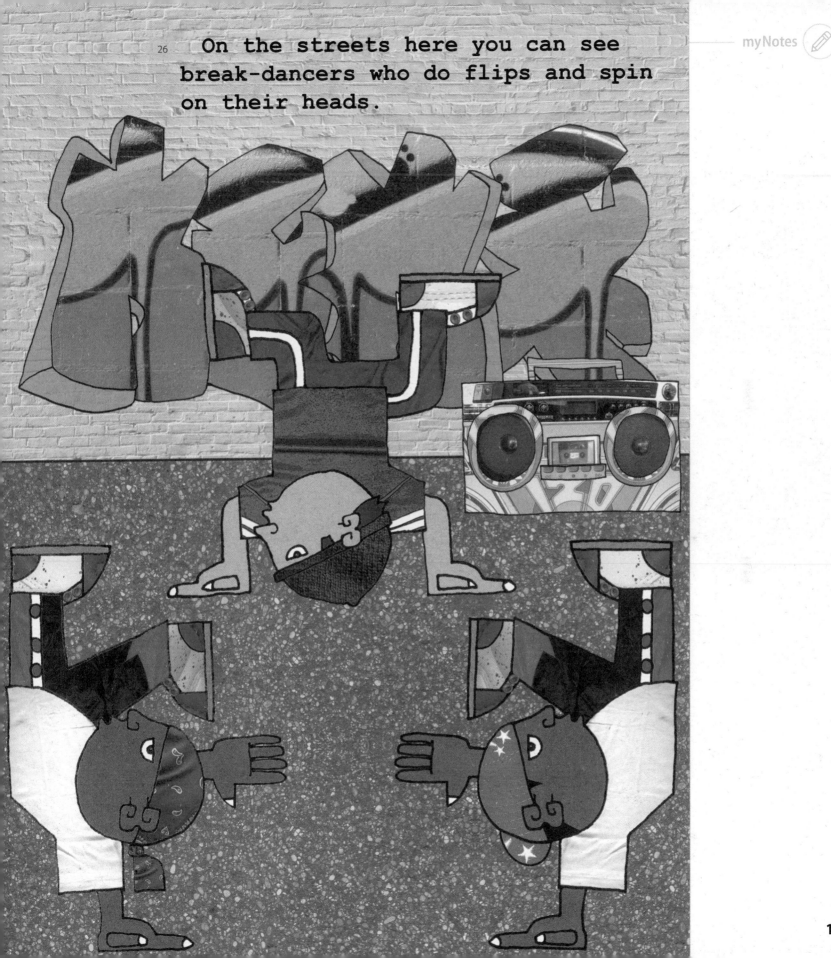

27 In Mexico we have so many traditions, such as the *Día de los Muertos,* the Day of the Dead.

28   My favorite tradition is attending the December parties called *Posadas*. At the end of each *Posada* there is a *piñata* filled with fruit and sweets. When someone breaks it, we all get to jump in.

piñata

29   In America we have traditions, too, such as Thanksgiving, when we eat turkey . . .

30   . . . and Halloween,
when we dress up and go
trick-or-treating. But I
have to stop writing now.
My mom just told me I
have to brush my teeth
and go to bed.

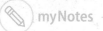

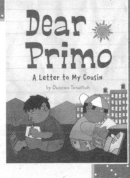

Collaborative Discussion

Look back at what you wrote on page 110. Tell a partner why your ideas were correct or incorrect. Then work with a group to discuss the questions below. Use details and examples from *Dear Primo* to support your answers. Take notes for your responses. Follow the rules for a polite discussion by being a good listener and by taking turns speaking.

1 Review pages 116–117. Why does Charlie explain what a subway is in his letter?

> Charlie explains a subway is so his cousin understans what it feels in like.

2 Reread pages 120–123. What does Carlitos usually do after school?

> After School carlitos Plays with his PaPalote, helps mom with dinner, and eats tortias.

3 What is one way the cousins' lives are alike? What is one way their lives are different? Give examples.

> There lives are alike because They both have traditions and There dificrent because they Play diferent SPorts.

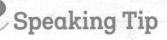

Listening Tip

Listen carefully to what each person in your group has to say. Look at the person who is speaking.

Speaking Tip

Don't start talking until the person before you has finished speaking. Be sure that everyone in your group has a chance to share his or her ideas.

Write a Response

Respond to the Text In *Dear Primo*, two cousins write letters to each other and share stories about their lives. Think about the words the author uses in the text to help you know the difference between Carlitos's writing and Charlie's writing. What words make each character's writing special? How do the characters express themselves in their writing? Cite evidence from the text to support your response.

EVIDENCE

List details from *Dear Primo* that show the difference between Carlitos's writing and Charlie's writing. Note how they each use different words to express themselves.

they write diferences in there lifes and the fonnts are diferent they explain the things they do are diferent

WRITE

Now write your response in a paragraph.

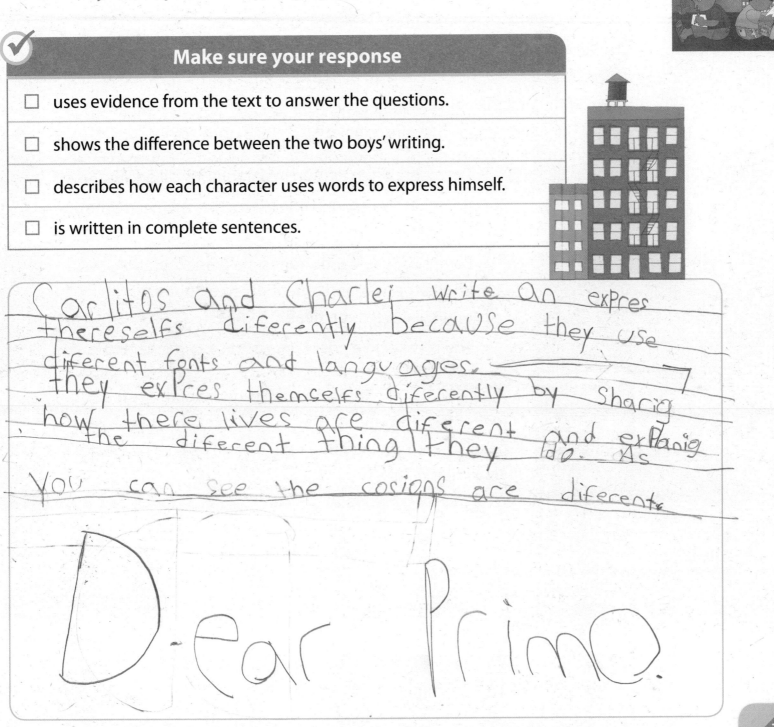

Make sure your response

☐ uses evidence from the text to answer the questions.

☐ shows the difference between the two boys' writing.

☐ describes how each character uses words to express himself.

☐ is written in complete sentences.

Carlitos and Charlei write an expres thereselfs diferently because they use diferent fonts and languages. they expres themselfs diferently by sharig how there lives are diferent and explanig the diferent thing they do. As you can see the cosigns are diferent.

Dear Primo.

Prepare to Read

GENRE STUDY **Poetry** uses the sounds and rhythms of words to show images and express feelings.

- Poems are often written in paragraphs called stanzas.
- Poems include sound effects, such as rhyme, rhythm, and meter.
- Poems include word sounds, such as alliteration, onomatopoeia, and repetition, to emphasize particular words or ideas.
- The speaker in a poem reflects on a particular topic.

SET A PURPOSE **Think about** the genre of this text and look at the illustrations. How do you think the poems will be different from the other texts you've read so far? Write your ideas below.

Poems are more shorter to read and books are longer.

CRITICAL VOCABULARY

desires

entry

Meet the Poets: Casie Hermansson and Eloise Greenfield

Adventures with Words

Thanks

I,
Like You

from
Cricket Magazine

by
Casie Hermansson
illustrated by
Susan Farrington

1 That smile on your face

is like a simile.

I don't know how it got there

but it looks just right.

5 It says you know I don't like

the same shade of blue as you,

but I'll agree with you anyway

because friends are like that.

Like a simile

10 your smile is nearly the same as mine,

but not quite:

Which is exactly how I like it.

There was an Old Man with a Beard

by Edward Lear

1 There was an Old Man with a beard

   Who said, "It is just as I feared!"

   Two Owls and a Hen,

   Four Larks and a Wren,

5 Have all built their nests in my beard!"

My Journal

1 I try to explain
   my heart's simple desires in
   a journal entry

desires Your desires are your wishes for certain things to happen.

entry If you write an entry, you write a short note in a diary or a book.

In the Land of Words

by Eloise Greenfield

illustrated by Jan Spivey Gilchrist

In the Land of Words

1 In the land
of words,
I stand as still
as a tree,
5 and let the words
rain down on me.
Come, rain, bring
your knowledge and your
music. Sing
10 while I grow green
and full.
I'll stand as still
as a tree,
and let your blessings
15 fall on me.

Jokes

1 Every day we get together
to see who can tell
the funniest joke.
We don't even have to vote.

5 It's always Crystal
who wins.
The words come flying
out of her mouth,
straight to the center
10 of our funny bones,
tickling us into
losing the game
and loving it.

Riddles

1 The ones I like the most
are the ones that make you
think and think,
while everybody waits,
5 hoping you'll give up.

Give up? Not me.
I'll get it.
You'll see.

I Go to the Land

1   I go to the land of words,
    for I am at home there,
    and never leave
    for long. My thirst
5   pushes me through
    the open door.
    The more I drink
    of the falling water,
    the more I know.
10 I drink. I think.

I grow.

Collaborative Discussion

Look back at what you wrote on page 144. Tell a partner two things that you noticed in *Adventures with Words*. Then work with a group to discuss the questions below. Explain your answers by using details from the selection of poems. Take notes for your responses and refer to them as you speak.

1 Reread "In the Land of Words." The poem uses a tree as a metaphor for the narrator. What helps the tree grow?

> the words rainig helps grow Knowlge.

Listening Tip

If you don't understand what a group member has said, wait until that person has finished talking. Then ask the speaker a question.

2 Review the poem on page 146. What messages can a smile send?

Speaking Tip

One way to check that you understand what someone else has said is to briefly retell his or her main points in your own words.

3 What do Eloise Greenfield's poems tell you about how she feels about words?

Write a Response

Respond to the Text All of the poems in *Adventures with Words* have one thing in common: they all celebrate words. What does each poem teach you about words? How does each poem make you feel about words? What words in the poems make you feel that way? Cite evidence from the text to support your response.

EVIDENCE

List details from the poems in *Adventures with Words* that tell what you learned about words and how they make you feel.

Now write your response in a paragraph.

✓	Make sure your response
☐	uses evidence from the poems.
☐	explains how the poems make you feel about words.
☐	is written in complete sentences.

decriptive W.
Words\ sensory
language
Words
Used to add
detail so the
reader can
imagine a
picture in
there mind.

Prepare to Read

GENRE STUDY   A **memoir** is a text about the personal experiences and memories of its author. A memoir may focus on one part of his or her life.

- Memoirs include events that happened in the past that are usually presented in chronological order.
- The events in a nonfiction memoir include real people and their feelings about those events.
- Authors of memoirs use descriptive language and sensory words to share their experiences.

SET A PURPOSE   **Think about** the title and genre of this text. Why do you think the author chose this title? What do you think the text will be about? Write your ideas.

CRITICAL VOCABULARY

steep

speed

breezy

conductor

**Meet the Author and Illustrator:
Juan Felipe Herrera and
Elizabeth Gómez**

The Upside Down Boy

story by **Juan Felipe Herrera**

illustrations by **Elizabeth Gómez**

1 When I was little, *my family spent years working in the fields as campesinos. One day, my mama said to my papi, "Let's settle down. It's time that Juanito goes to school." That year we were living in the mountains by Lake Wolfer, a glassy world full of sky colors.*

2 *Papi's old army truck brought us down the steep mountain roads, all the way to Mrs. Andasola's pink house on Juniper Street. I was eight years old and about to live in a big city for the first time.*

—Juan Felipe Herrera

steep   If a hill or a mountain is steep, it is difficult to climb because it goes almost straight up.

3   Mama, who loves words, sings out the name on the
street sign—Juniper. "Who-nee-purr! Who-nee-purr!"

4   Papi parks our old army truck on Juniper Street
in front of Mrs. Andasola's tiny pink house.
"We found it at last," Papi shouts, "Who-nee-purr!"

5   "Time to start school," Mama tells me with music in her voice.
"My Who-nee-purr Street!" I yell to the chickens in the yard.

6 "Don't worry, *chico*,"
Papi says as he walks me to school.
"Everything changes. A new place has new leaves
on the trees and blows fresh air into your body."

7 I pinch my ear. Am I really here?
Maybe the street lamp is really a golden cornstalk
with a dusty gray coat.

8 People speed by alone in their fancy melting cars.
In the valleys, campesinos sang "*Buenos días*, Juanito."

9 I make a clown face, half funny,
half scared. "I don't speak English," I say to Papi.
"Will my tongue turn into a rock?"

> **speed**   If you speed, you move too fast.

10 I slow step into school.
My *burrito de papas*, my potato burrito in a brown bag.
Empty playground,
fences locked. One cloud up high.

11 No one
in the halls. Open a door with a blue number 27.
"*¿Dónde estoy?*" Where am I?
My question in Spanish fades
as the thick door slams behind me.

12 Mrs. Sampson, the teacher, shows me my desk.
Kids laugh when I poke my nose into my lunch bag.

13 The hard round clock above my head
clicks and aims its strange arrows at me.

14   On the chalkboard, I see a row
of alphabet letters and addition numbers. If I learn them
will they grow like seeds?

15   If I learn the English words
will my voice reach the ceiling, weave through it
like grape vines?

16   We are finger-painting.
I make wild suns with my open hands.
Crazy tomato cars and cucumber sombreros—
I write my name with seven chiles.

17   "What is that?" Mrs. Sampson asks.
My tongue is a rock.

18   The school bell rings
and shakes me.

19   I run and grab my lunch bag
and sit on the green steel bench.
In a few fast minutes, I finish my potato burrito.
But everyone plays,
and I am alone.

20   "It is only recess,"
my classmate Amanda says in Spanish.
In Spanish, I pronounce "recess" slowly.
"Sounds like '*reses*'—like the word for cattle,
huh?" I say.

21   "What is recess?" I ask Amanda.

22   The high bell
roars again.

23   This time everyone eats their sandwiches
while I play in the breezy baseball diamond
by myself.

24   "Is this recess?" I ask again.

25   When I jump up
everyone sits.
When I sit
all the kids swing through the air.
My feet float through the clouds
when all I want is to touch the earth.
I am the upside down boy.

breezy   When it is breezy outside, you can feel
the wind softly blowing.

26 Papi comes home to Mrs. Andasola's pink house.
I show him my finger painting.
"What a spicy sun," he sings out.
"It reminds me of hot summer days in the San Joaquin Valley,"
he says, brushing his dark hair with his hands.

27 "Look, mama!
See my painting?"

28 "Those are flying tomatoes
ready for salsa," Mama sings.
She shows my painting to Mrs. Andasola
who shows it to Gabino, her canary.

29 "Gabino, Gabino, see?" Mrs. Andasola yells.
"What do you think?"
Gabino nods his head back and forth.
"Pío, pío, piiiii!"

30 Mrs. Sampson invites me
to the front of the class. "Sing, Juanito,
sing a song we have been practicing."

31 I pop up shaking. I am alone facing the class.

32 "Ready to sing?" Mrs. Sampson asks me.
I am frozen, then a deep breath fills me,
"Three blind mice, three blind mice," I sing.

33 My eyes open as big as the ceiling and
my hands spread out as if catching
rain drops from the sky.

34 "You have a very beautiful voice, Juanito," Mrs. Sampson says.
"What is beautiful?" I ask Amanda after school.

35 At home, I help Mama and Mrs. Andasola
make *buñuelos*—fried sweet cinnamon tortilla chips.

36 "Piiiiicho, come heeeere," I sing out,
calling my dog as I stretch a dough ball.

37 "Listen to meeeee," I sing to Picho with his ears
curled up into fuzzy triangles. "My voice is beauuuuutiful!"

38 "What is he singing?" Mrs. Andasola asks my mom
as she gently lays a buñuelo into the frying pan.

39 "My teacher says my voice is beauuuuutiful," I sing,
dancing with a tiny dough ball stuck on my nose.

40 "*Sí, sí*," Mama laughs.
"Let's see if your buñuelos come out beautiful too."

41 “I only made it to the third grade, Juanito,”
Mama tells me as I get ready for bed.

42 “When we lived in El Paso, Texas,
my mother needed help at home. We were very poor
and she was tired from cleaning people's houses.”

43 “That year your mama won a spelling medal,”
Papi says as he shaves in the bathroom.

44 “Your Papi learned English without a school,” Mama says.
“When he worked the railroads, he would pay
his buddies a penny for each word they taught him.”

45 Papi says softly, “Each word,
each language has its own magic.”

46 After a week of reading a new poem aloud to us every day
Mrs. Sampson says, "Write a poem,"
as she plays symphony music on the old red phonograph.

47 I think of Mama, squeeze my pencil,
pour letters from the shiny tip like a skinny river.

48 The waves tumble onto the page.
L's curl at the bottom.
F's tip their hats from their heads.
M's are sea waves. They crash over my table.

Juanito's Poem

49

Papi Felipe with a mustache of words.
Mama Lucha with strawberries in her hair.
I see magic salsa in my house and everywhere!

50   "I got an A on my poem!" I yell to everyone
in the front yard where Mama gives Papi a haircut.

51   I show Gabino my paper
as I fly through the kitchen to the backyard.

52   "Listen," I sing to the baby chicks,
with my hands up as if I am a famous music conductor.

53   I sprinkle corn kernels and sing out my poem.
Each fuzzy chick gets a name:
"Beethoven! You are the one with the bushy head!
Mozart! You jumpy black-spotted hen!
Johann Sebastian! Tiny red rooster, dance, dance!"

> **conductor** A conductor directs a group of people who sing or play musical instruments.

171

54 In the morning, as we walk to school
Papi turns and says, "You do have a nice voice, Juanito.
I never heard you sing until yesterday
when you fed the chickens.
At first, when we moved here,
you looked sad and I didn't know what to do."

55 "I felt funny, upside down," I say to him.
"The city streets aren't soft with flowers.
Buildings don't have faces. You know, Papi,
in the campo I knew all the names, even of those bugs
with little wild eyes and shiny noses!"

56 "Here," he says. "Here's my harmonica.
It has many voices, many beautiful songs
just like you. Sing them!"

57 On Open House Day,
Mama and Papi sit in the front row.
Mrs. Andasola admires our drawings on the walls,
Gabino on her shoulder.

58 "Our paintings look like the flowery fields back
in the Valley," I tell Amanda.

59 "I have a surprise," I whisper to Mama.
"I am '*El Maestro* Juanito,' the choir conductor!"
Mrs. Sampson smiles wearing a chile sombrero
and puts on the music.

60 I blow a "C" with my harmonica—"La la la laaaaah!
Ready to sing out your poems?" I ask my choir.
"*Uno . . . dos . . .* and three!"

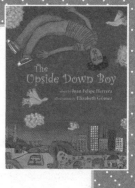

Collaborative Discussion

Look back at what you wrote on page 154. Tell a partner why you thought the author used the title *The Upside Down Boy*. Then work with a group to discuss the questions below. Refer to details and examples in *The Upside Down Boy* to support your ideas. Take notes for your responses and use them as you speak. As you share your ideas, be sure to speak clearly and in a way that everyone can understand.

1. Reread page 158. Why does the author worry that his tongue will "turn into a rock"?

2. Reread pages 165–166. What does Mrs. Sampson invite Juanito to do? How does this help him?

3. Why does Juanito call himself "the upside down boy"? What seems upside down to him?

Listening Tip

As you listen, think about how you can add to the discussion. Plan what you want to say about each question.

Speaking Tip

Use complete sentences. Speak loudly enough so that everyone in the group can hear.

Write a Response

PROMPT

Respond to the Text The author of *The Upside Down Boy* writes about an important time in his life. He describes his feelings and all the things that are new to him. What words does the author use to help you understand how he feels? What words does he use to make his writing special or to show his voice? Cite evidence from the text to support your response.

EVIDENCE

List details from *The Upside Down Boy* that tell how the author feels and show his voice.

WRITE

Now write your response in a paragraph.

Make sure your response
☐ answers the questions.
☐ uses evidence from the text.
☐ explains the author's feelings.
☐ describes how the author makes his writing special or shows his voice.
☐ is written in complete sentences.

Notice &
Note
Aha Moment

Prepare to Read

GENRE STUDY **Fantasies** are imaginative stories with characters and events that could not be real. **Letters** are written messages from one person to another. **Poetry** uses the sounds and rhythms of words to show images and express feelings.

- Fantasies often include events that do not follow the laws of nature and time.
- Letters begin with a greeting and end with a closing.
- Poems use descriptive language and often rhyme.

SET A PURPOSE **Think about** the title and genres of this text. What do you think makes this story a fantasy? Why do you think this story includes letters? How might it include poetry? Write your ideas below.

Meet the Author and Illustrator:
Josh Funk and Rodolfo Montalvo

CRITICAL VOCABULARY

projects

assigned

mosaics

retains

precious

demolition

dear DRAGON

written by
Josh Funk

illustrated by
Rodolfo Montalvo

1 Hello, students!
2 Our poetry and pen pal projects
    this year are combined.
3 Upon your desks you'll see the pen pals
    that you've been assigned.

projects   Projects are tasks that take time and effort to complete.

assigned   If someone assigned a task to you, he or she gave you some work to do.

4 Please make sure the letters that you
  write are all in rhyme.

5 Now open up your envelopes because
  it's pen pal time!

September 12th

Dear Blaise Dragomir,

6 We haven't met each other, and I don't know what to say.

7 I really don't like writing, but I'll do it anyway.

8 Yesterday my dad and I designed a giant fort.

9 I like playing catch and soccer. What's your favorite sport?

Sincerely,
George Slair

October 1st

Dear George Slair,

10   I also don't like writing, but I'll try it, I suppose.

11   A fort is like a castle, right? I love attacking those.

12   My favorite sport is skydiving. I jump near Falcor Peak.

13   Tomorrow is my birthday but my party is next week.

Sincerely,
Blaise Dragomir

October 31st

Dear Blaise Dragomir,

14 You know how to skydive? That's as awesome as it gets!

15 My dog destroyed my fort last night. Do you have any pets?

16 Happy birthday, by the way! I don't have mine till June.

17 I'm trick-or-treating as a knight. We're heading out real soon.

George Slair

November 14th

Dear George Slair,

18 Knights are super-scary! I don't like to trick-or-treat.

19 Brushing teeth is such a pain, I rarely eat a sweet.

20 My pet's a Bengal kitten and tonight she needs a bath.

21 What's your favorite class in school? I'm really into math!

Blaise Dragomir

December 16th

Dear Blaise D.,

22 My favorite class is art. I made
    a mold of my left hand.

23 Next we'll craft mosaics using
    pebbles, stones, and sand.

24 Yesterday I won a prize in
    this year's science fair.

25 My towering volcano blasted
    lava everywhere!

George S.

mosaics Mosaics are pictures or patterns made from smaller pieces of glass, stone, or other materials.

192

193

January 18th

Dear George S.,

26 My father's won our local fire-breathing contest twice.

27 He still retains the record, melting fifty cubes of ice.

28 Do you have any hobbies? I enjoy collecting rocks.

29 I keep them in a secret place inside a precious box.

Blaise D.

retains If someone retains something, he or she has something and keeps it.

precious If something is precious to you, it is important or valuable to you.

February 22nd

Blaise,

30 Fire breathing? What's your father's job? My folks are teachers.

31 I collect exotic monsters, animals, and creatures.

32 Oh, guess what! I heard the news this morning from Miss Sweet.

33 A pen pal picnic's planned for June! At last we'll get to meet!

George

March 15th

George,

34 Dad's in demolition. He works
   hard throughout the day.

35 But every night we read a book
   or pick a game to play.

36 Soon he's gonna take me flying,
   once it's really spring.

37 It's such a rush to ride the air
   that flows from wing to wing.

Blaise

demolition If you work in demolition, your job
is to tear down or destroy buildings.

April 11th

Hi, Blaise!

38 Skydiving <u>and</u> flying lessons? Wow, your parents rock!

39 I'm lucky if my father lets me bike around the block.

40 Once the school year's over and this project is complete,

41 should we continue writing? 'Cause it could be kind of neat. . . .

Your friend, George

May 12th

Hey, George!

42 I'm psyched about the picnic and
    I can't wait to attend.

43 Who'd have thought this pen pal
    thing would make me a new friend?

44 Writing more sounds awesome.
    I was gonna ask you, too!

45 I've never liked to write as much
    as when I write to you.

Your friend, Blaise

46 **"Blaise?"**

47 "George?"

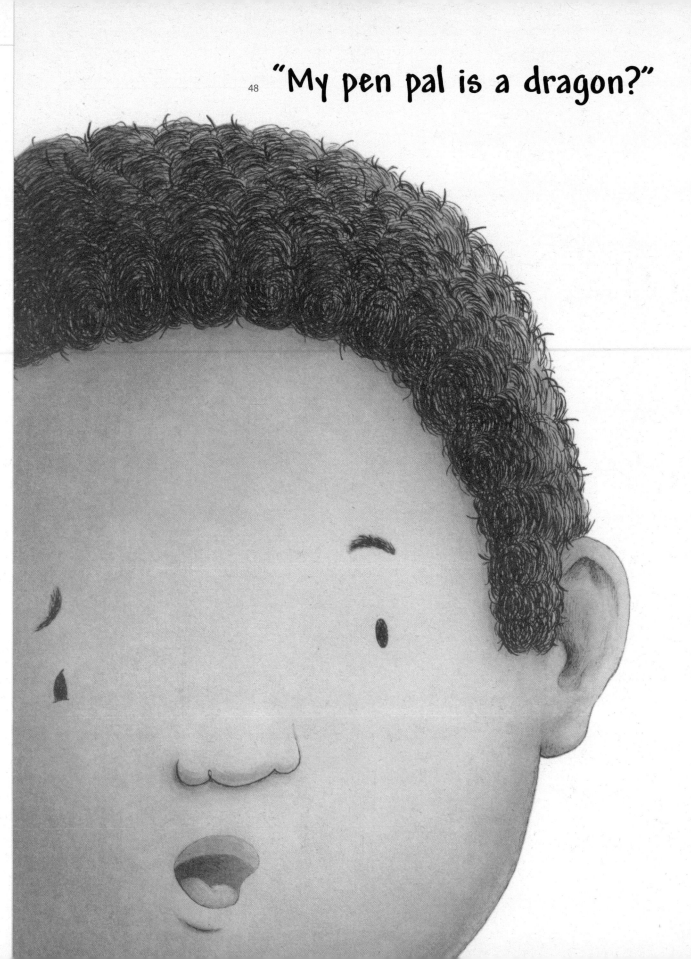

"My pen pal is a dragon?"

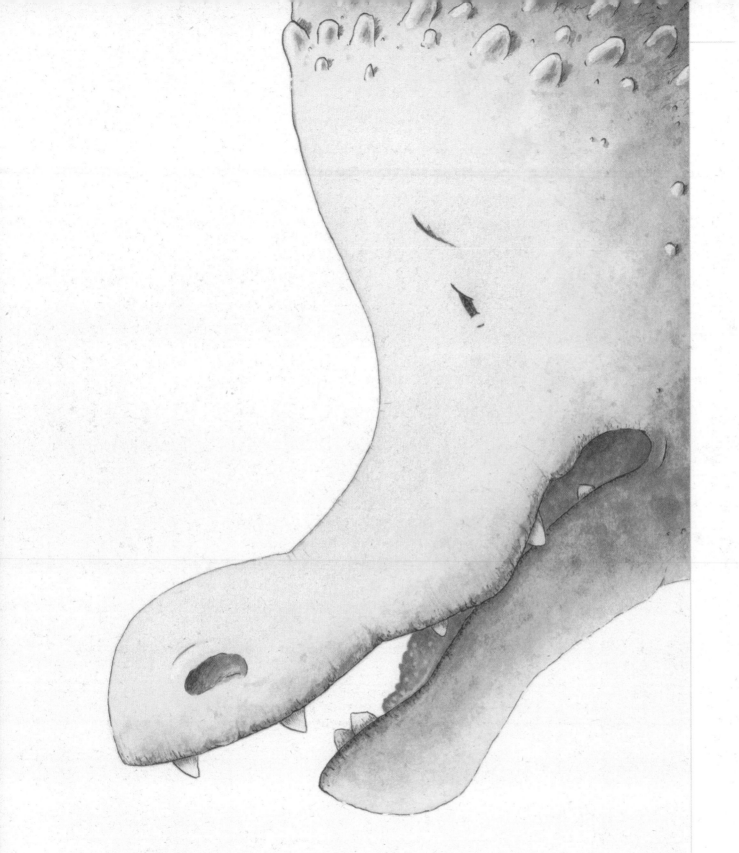

49 "My pen pal is a human?"

50   "Our plan was a success, my friend,
      or so it would appear!"

51   "The Poetry and Pen Pal Project!
      Once again next year?"

Collaborative Discussion

Look back at what you wrote on page 178. Work with a group to discuss the questions below. Refer to details and examples from *Dear Dragon* to support your answers. Take notes for your responses. Follow the rules for a polite discussion by being a good listener and by taking turns speaking.

1. Review pages 184–199. Why does each pen pal picture show something different than the letter writer meant?

2. Review pages 204–205. What can you tell about how George and Blaise feel when they first see one another?

3. How do the pen pal letters change as time passes?

Listening Tip

As you listen, think about new ideas you can share. Jot down some notes about what you would like to tell your group.

Speaking Tip

Work with your group to make sure everyone gets a chance to speak. Make sure you look at others while you speak and respect what they have to say.

Write a Response

PROMPT

Respond to the Text *Dear Dragon* tells the story of two pen pals who write letters to one another over the course of a school year. What do you learn about each character from the words they use in their letters? How do the words they use help you understand how they feel about each other and themselves? Cite evidence from the text to support your response.

EVIDENCE

List details from *Dear Dragon* that describe each character and how they feel about each other and about themselves.

WRITE

Now write your response in a paragraph.

Make sure your response

- ☐ answers the questions.
- ☐ uses evidence from the text.
- ☐ describes each character.
- ☐ explains how the characters feel about each other and themselves.
- ☐ is written in complete sentences.

(?) Essential Question

How do people use words to express themselves?

Write an Opinion Essay

PROMPT Think about the selections you read in this module. How did the authors and poets use words to express themselves? What kind of impact did the words have on you? Write an opinion essay about whether or not you think that words matter. Use evidence from the module selections to support your opinion.

Make sure your opinion essay
☐ states your opinion clearly.
☐ includes reasons supported by evidence and examples from the texts.
☐ uses transition words and phrases, such as *because* and *in addition*.
☐ sums up your opinion in a conclusion.

Think about how you felt as you read each selection in the module. What words did the authors use that made you feel that way? Think about whether or not the author's word choice is important. Use the map below to plan your writing.

Opinion

Reason 1	Reason 2	Reason 3

DRAFT · Write your opinion essay.

Use the information you wrote on page 215 to draft your essay. Write an
introduction that states your opinion about whether or not words matter.

Write a paragraph that includes the reasons and text evidence that
support your opinion. Present your reasons in an order that makes sense,
including transition words and phrases.

Conclude your essay by restating your opinion.

The revising and editing steps give you a chance to look carefully at your writing and make changes. Work with a partner to determine whether you have explained your ideas clearly. Use the questions below to help you.

PURPOSE/ FOCUS	ORGANIZATION	EVIDENCE/ SUPPORT	ELABORATION	CONVENTIONS
☐ Does my essay answer the questions? ☐ Do I explain my opinion about whether or not words matter?	☐ Do I explain my reasons in an order that makes sense? ☐ Does my conclusion restate my opinion?	☐ Do I include text evidence and examples from the selections?	☐ Do I use words such as *because* to connect my opinion and reasons? ☐ Do I use clear and exact words to explain my reasons?	☐ Have I spelled all words correctly? ☐ Have I used correct punctuation and capitalization? ☐ Have I indented each paragraph?

PUBLISH ·· Create a finished copy.

Make a final copy of your opinion essay. Use your cursive writing skills.

Let Freedom Ring!

"I love to see the starry flag
That floats above my head.
I love to see its wavering folds
With stripes of white and red."

—from "Our Flag"

How do historic places, documents, and symbols represent our nation?

Get Curious
Video

Historic Documents

America

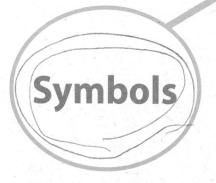

Symbols

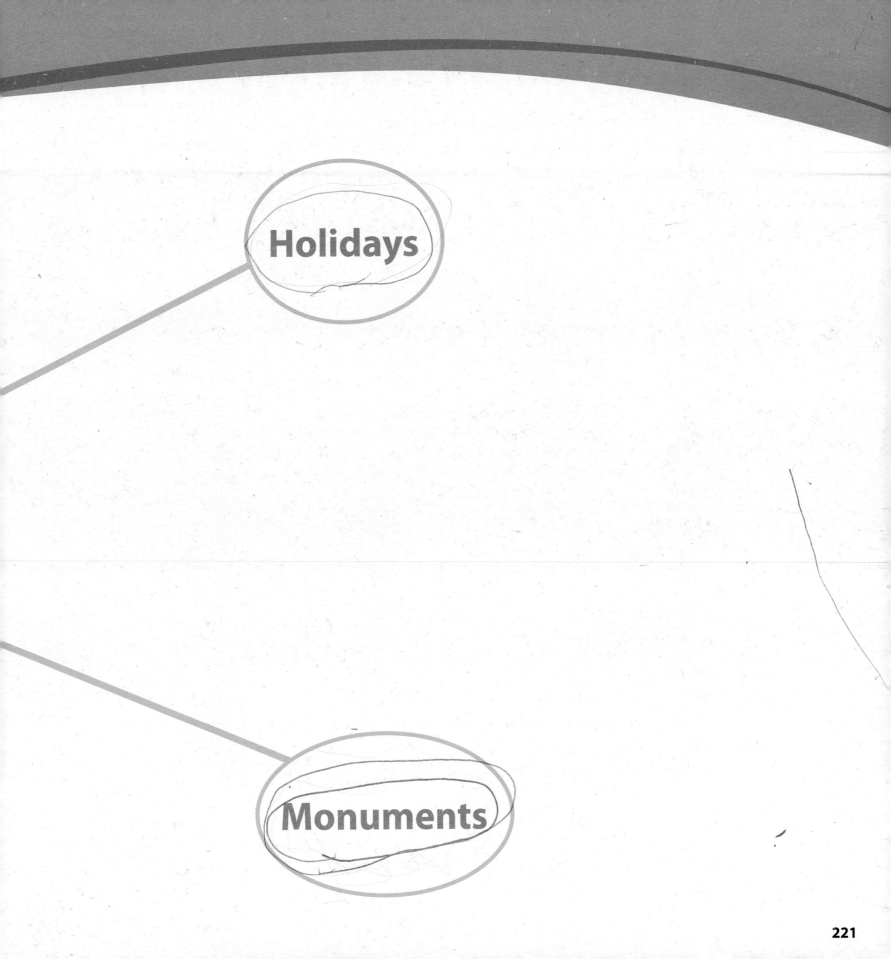

Holidays

Monuments

AMERICAN PLACES, AMERICAN IDEALS

loyal When you are loyal to someone or something, you strongly support it.

sovereignty Sovereignty is the right and power a nation has to rule itself or another country or state.

democracy A democracy is a kind of government in which the people choose leaders by voting.

civic The word *civic* describes the duties, rights, and responsibilities of citizens in a community, city, or nation.

1 *Americans are loyal to the idea of freedom. In fact, our country was founded on it. Washington, D.C., our nation's capital, stands for this important ideal. This map shows sites in Washington, D.C., that stand for freedom.*

The Lincoln Memorial

2 Abraham Lincoln was our 16th president. Lincoln led our country through the American Civil War, from 1861 to 1865.

3 The Lincoln Memorial was finished in 1922. The memorial holds a statue of Lincoln, and his Gettysburg Address is inscribed on one wall. The memorial honors Lincoln and his ideals of freedom and justice.

The Jefferson Memorial

4 Thomas Jefferson was our third president. He wrote the first draft of the Declaration of Independence. It said the United States of America was free from Great Britain's sovereignty, or rule.

5 The Jefferson Memorial was finished in 1943. It holds a statue of Jefferson looking toward the White House. Words from the Declaration of Independence are carved into the southwest wall.

myNotes

The decloration lets all new kinds of people

The washington mounment is a tributo to George washington

The White House

6   Construction of the White House began in 1792. After eight years, the house was ready for President John Adams and his wife, Abigail, to move in. The White House has been called many different names, including the "President's Palace," but in 1901, President Theodore Roosevelt officially gave it its current name.

7   The White House is a symbol of democracy. Democracy means "rule by the people." That's how our government works. We are free to choose our leaders by voting.

The Washington Monument

8   The Washington Monument was finished in 1884. It honors the first United States president, George Washington. He fought for our freedom from Great Britain. The Washington Monument is the tallest building in Washington. It always will be, too.

The United States Capitol

9   The United States Capitol was first built in 1800. Congress meets there to make laws. This civic responsibility is so important that citizens from all 50 states elect the members of Congress. Through Congress, all citizens help shape our country's future.

10   On the Capitol dome stands the Statue of Freedom. This bronze figure of a woman wears a helmet. The helmet symbolizes her role as a protector of American values.

Prepare to Read

GENRE STUDY **Informational texts** give facts and examples about a topic.

- Informational texts often include headings and subheadings to signal what comes next.
- Informational texts include central ideas supported by key details and facts.
- Informational texts may include social studies words specific to the topic.
- Informational texts include visuals and text features.

SET A PURPOSE **Think about** the title and genre of this text. What do you know about the U.S. Constitution? What might you learn? Write your ideas below.

**Meet the Author and Illustrator:
Norman Pearl and Matthew Skeens**

CRITICAL VOCABULARY

convention

delegates

domestic

welfare

posterity

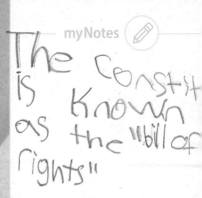

The constit is known as the "bill of rights"

The U.S. Constitution

by **Norman Pearl**

illustrated by
Matthew Skeens

1 My name is James Madison.
I was the fourth president of the United States. I also
played a big part in making a set of rules for the
country. These rules are known as the Constitution.
Let me tell you the story.

What is the U.S. Constitution?

2 The Constitution of the United States is the plan for how the government works. It says how much power the branches, or parts, of the government can have. It tells them how to make laws and how to make sure all Americans follow them. The Constitution is a symbol of democracy.

> The Constitution is the highest law in the United States. It is more important than any city or state law.

The First Rules of the United States

3 After winning the Revolutionary War in 1783, the United States was a new country. Like any country, it needed rules. Its first set of rules was called the Articles of Confederation. These rules joined together the 13 states.

4 It was a start, but the country needed more. The United States needed a better form of government.

Rhode Island was the only state that did not send any delegates to the Constitutional Convention.

Who wrote the Constitution?

5   In May 1787, delegates from most of the 13 states met in Philadelphia, Pennsylvania. Their job was to write the Constitution, a new set of rules for the country's government.

6   The meeting was called the Constitutional Convention. The 55 delegates at the meeting later became known as the Framers of the Constitution.

convention   A convention is a meeting of people who share the same purpose or ideas.

delegates   People who have been chosen to make decisions for a larger group are called delegates.

Many Different Ideas

7   Writing the Constitution was not easy. Many people had different ideas about what it should say. Some men wanted a strong national government. Others did not. There was a lot of arguing.

8   Finally, on September 17, 1787, the arguing stopped, and the delegates signed the Constitution. Then the states had to agree to follow it. The last one did so in 1790.

James Madison was a delegate from Virginia. He helped the other delegates at the Constitutional Convention work through their differences. Madison was both smart and fair. He is known today as the Father of the Constitution.

The Parts of the Constitution

9 The Constitution has three main parts: the preamble, the articles, and the amendments.

1. PREAMBLE

10 The preamble is the beginning of the Constitution. The preamble tells Americans why they need a government and a Constitution.

11 *We the People of the United States, in Order to form a more perfect Union, establish Justice, insure domestic Tranquility, provide for the common defense, promote the general Welfare, and secure the Blessings of Liberty to ourselves and our Posterity, do ordain and establish this Constitution for the United States of America.*

domestic   When something is domestic, it is a part of or about the country in which you live.

welfare   If someone looks out for your welfare, that person makes sure you are healthy and happy.

posterity   If you think ahead to all the people who will be alive in the future, you are thinking about posterity.

The articles allow people in government to keep all Americans safe. They say that the government can build an army and a navy to guard the country.

2. ARTICLES

12 The seven articles of the Constitution explain the branches of the U.S. government. They tell what those branches can and cannot do. In the United States, the people run the government. Americans have the right to vote. When they vote, Americans choose the people who will work for them in the government.

13 The articles divide the U.S. government into three branches. Each branch has different powers. No one branch can become stronger than the others. This is called a "balance of power." Every branch is equal.

The Executive Branch

14 This branch is made up of the president, the vice president, and the people who help them do their jobs. It is headquartered in the White House.

The Judicial Branch

15 This branch is the court system. Judges see that laws are carried out in the right way. The Judicial Branch is headquartered in the Supreme Court, the highest court in the United States.

Supreme Court

White House

The Judicial Branch

Capitol

The Executive Branch

The Legislative Branch

The Legislative Branch

16 This branch is made up of the Congress, which is divided into two parts: the House of Representatives and the Senate. Congress makes the nation's laws. It is headquartered in the Capitol.

3. AMENDMENTS

17   The amendments were not part of the original Constitution. They were added later. They give Americans many rights. For example, the amendments say that Americans cannot be made slaves. They can belong to any religion they want. All Americans age 18 and older can vote. Since it was signed in 1787, the Constitution has been amended, or added to, 27 times. The first 10 amendments are called the Bill of Rights. These are the most important rights Americans have.

The Constitution and You

18 So, how does the Constitution work for you? The Constitution gives the U.S. government the power to make laws. Laws aren't just for adults. They're for kids, too.

19 There are laws that allow kids to go to school. Others say what kinds of jobs kids can have and how many hours they can work.

20 For more than 200 years, the Constitution has kept the U.S. government strong. I'm proud of our Constitution. Now that you know its story, I hope you are, too!

You can see the original Constitution at the National Archives Building in Washington, D.C. The Bill of Rights and the Declaration of Independence are there, too.

Collaborative Discussion

Look back at what you wrote on page 224. Tell a partner two things you learned from the text. Work with a group to discuss the questions below. Refer to examples in *The U.S. Constitution* to support your ideas. Take notes and use them to respond.

1. Review page 229. Why is James Madison called the "Father of the Constitution"?

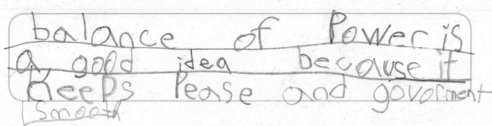

James madison is called father of the consituion becase he helped delicates work through diferences

2. Reread pages 231–232. What makes the "balance of power" a good idea for the U.S. government?

balance of power is a good idea because it keeps pease and goverment smooth

3. Reread page 234. Why is the Constitution important for young people?

The constitulion is important for young people because there are laws for kids to go to school and learn

Listening Tip

Listen closely to other speakers. If an idea is unclear or you need more information, prepare questions to get more details.

Speaking Tip

Share your ideas clearly. Be ready to answer questions others may have about what you have said.

Write a Response

PROMPT ·

Respond to the Text You read about the history of our laws and government in *The U.S. Constitution*. What kind of document is the Constitution? Why is this document important to our nation? Cite evidence from the text to support your response.

EVIDENCE ·

List ideas from *The U.S. Constitution* that help you understand why the Constitution is important to our nation.

WRITE

Now write your response in a paragraph.

Make sure your response

- ☐ answers the questions.
- ☐ uses evidence from the text.
- ☐ tells what the Constitution is and why it is important to our nation.
- ☐ is written in complete sentences.

Prepare to View

GENRE STUDY **Informational videos** present facts and information about a topic in a visual and audio form.

- A narrator explains what is happening on the screen.
- Real people and places are in the video.
- Informational videos may include words that are specific to a social studies topic.
- Producers of videos may include sound effects or music to make the video more interesting.

SET A PURPOSE **Think about** the title and genre of this video. What do you think you'll learn from the video? Write your ideas below.

Build Background: What Is a Democracy?

CRITICAL VOCABULARY

independence

declaring

endowed

presented

Why We Celebrate the Fourth of July

As you watch *Why We Celebrate the Fourth of July*, pay attention to the events that led to America becoming an independent country. Notice the images that are used to show events in the past. How do the images help you understand these important events? Takes notes in the space below.

As you watch, listen for the Critical Vocabulary words *independence, presented, declaring,* and *endowed* and for clues to the meaning of each word. Take notes in the space below about how each word is used.

independence   If you are free to set your own rules and make your own choices, you have independence.
presented   If you presented something, you showed it or gave it to someone.
declaring   When you are declaring something, you feel strongly about it and are making it clearly known.
endowed   If you have been endowed with a feature or quality, it is yours and belongs to you.

Collaborative Discussion

Work with a group to discuss the questions below. Refer to details and examples in *Why We Celebrate the Fourth of July* to support your ideas. Take notes for your responses and use them as you speak. During the discussion, listen actively by paying attention to the speakers.

1 What was the reason for writing the Declaration of Independence?

2 What are some of the ideas stated in the Declaration of Independence?

3 Why is the Fourth of July sometimes called America's birthday?

Listening Tip

Listen to make sure the speaker is staying on topic. If the discussion seems to be going in the wrong direction, ask questions to move it back on topic.

Speaking Tip

When it is your turn to speak, the ideas you share should be about the topic you are discussing.

Write a Response

PROMPT ....

Respond to the Video You learned about a national holiday in the video *Why We Celebrate the Fourth of July*. What do we celebrate on this day? Why is this holiday important to our nation? Cite evidence from the video to support your response.

EVIDENCE ....

List details from the video *Why We Celebrate the Fourth of July* that explain what we celebrate and why it is important to our nation.

Why We Celebrate the Fourth of July

WRITE

Now write your response in a paragraph.

✓ Make sure your response
☐ uses evidence from the video to answer the questions.
☐ explains why we celebrate the Fourth of July.
☐ tells why this holiday is important to our nation.
☐ is written in complete sentences.

Prepare to Read

GENRE STUDY ▸ **Narrative nonfiction** gives factual information by telling a true story.

- Narrative nonfiction includes real people and events and shows those events in chronological order.

- Narrative nonfiction may include words that are specific to the topic.

- Narrative nonfiction may include visuals.

SET A PURPOSE ▸ **Think about** the genre and title of this text. What do you know about the American flag? What do you want to learn? Write your ideas below.

The 50 stars stand for the 50 states. I want to learn that if the red and white and red stripes stand for anything.

Meet the Author and Illustrator:
Susan Campbell Bartoletti and Claire A. Nivola

CRITICAL VOCABULARY

broad

gritty

hoisted

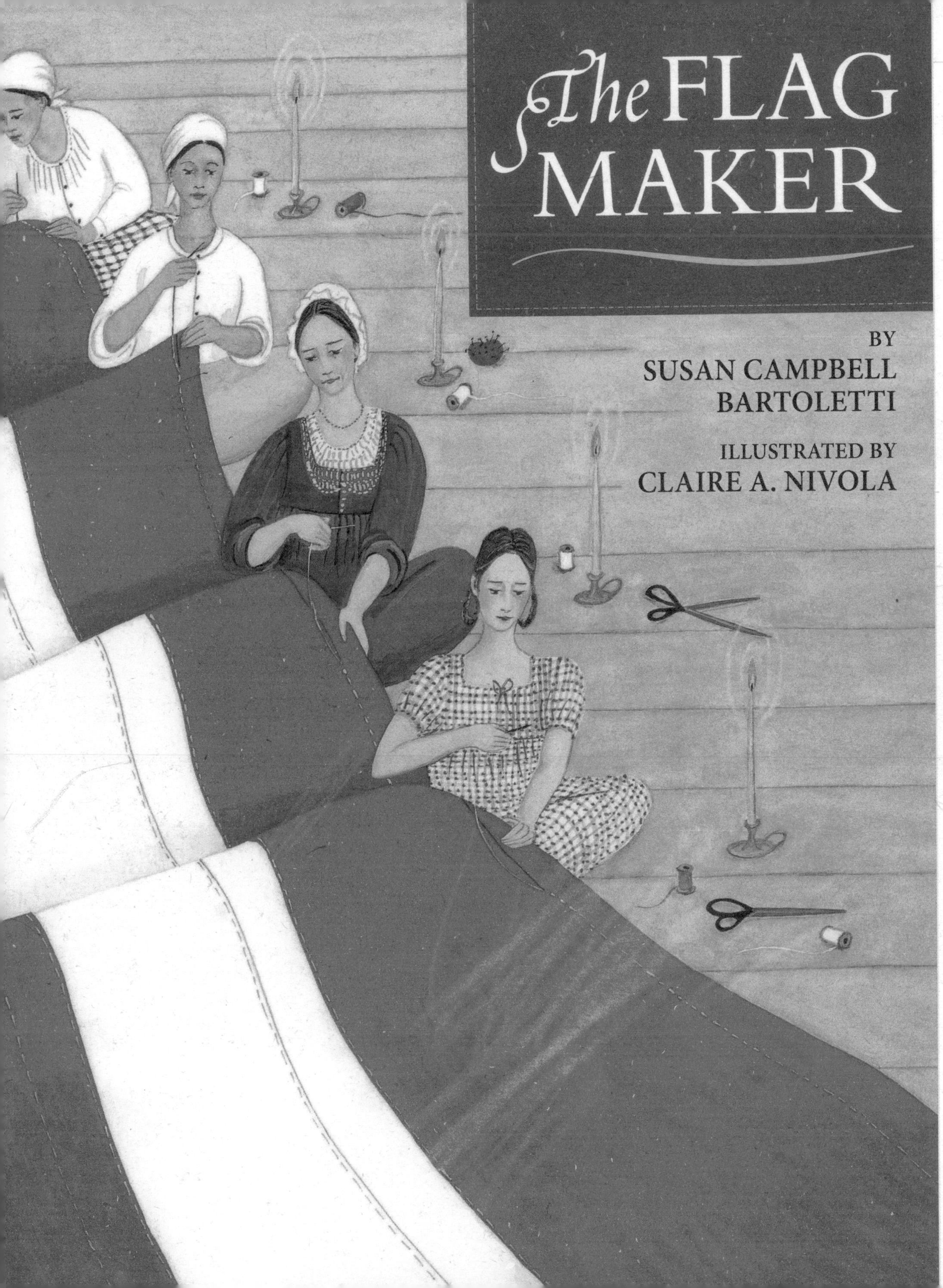

The FLAG MAKER

BY
SUSAN CAMPBELL
BARTOLETTI

ILLUSTRATED BY
CLAIRE A. NIVOLA

--- ★ ---

1   *It was 1812*, and the United States was at war with Britain. A country at war needed plenty of flags.

2   In Baltimore, a twelve-year-old girl named Caroline Pickersgill and her mother, Mary, made flags.

3   Caroline and her mother sewed flags so that militia and cavalry officers could direct their men during battles on land.

4   They sewed flags so that navy ships could communicate with each other during battles at sea.

5   They sewed flags for the privateers that attacked British ships.

6   But no matter how many flags they made and no matter how many battles the Americans fought, the Americans could not defeat the British.

--- ★ ---

7   One summer day, Caroline and her mother welcomed three military officers to their flag shop. The men ordered an American flag for Fort McHenry, the fort guarding the waters near Baltimore.

8   "The flag must be so large that the British will have no trouble seeing it from a distance," said one officer.

9   Excited, Caroline and her mother set to work right away. Out of wool bunting, they cut pieces for broad red and white stripes.

10   They cut a large field of dark blue.

11   They cut white cotton stars.

broad   Something that is broad is wide.

12 Day after day, they sewed stitch after stitch, red stripe after white stripe, star after star.

13 Caroline's grandmother and cousins helped.

14 So did her mother's slave.

15 Her house servant, too.

16 Night after night, they worked by candlelight, long past bedtime.

17 The wool bunting itched.

18 The needle pricked.

19 Caroline's fingers ached, and her eyes felt gritty and sore.

20 But, inch by inch, they sewed until the flag spilled over their laps and lay in folds on the floor.

gritty   When something feels gritty, it feels rough and sandy.

21   Soon the flag outgrew the sewing room. They carried it to a large malt house.

22   They spread out the flag on the malt house floor.

23   And they sewed still more.

24 Finally, after six long weeks, the last star was sewn into place.

25 The last threads were snipped and knotted.

26 From hoist to fly, it was the largest flag Caroline had ever seen.

27   The flag was delivered to Fort McHenry, where soldiers raised it high above the ramparts.

28   Each day Caroline looked for her flag as it waved over the fort. It looked tiny in the distance, but she felt proud.

29 Over the next year, the flag shop grew even busier.

30 Caroline and her mother sewed more flags.

31 The Americans fought more battles.

32 Yet they could not defeat the British, once and for all.

33 And so a difficult year passed.

34   Early one August morning, a horse clattered down the Baltimore streets. "British sails!" its rider shouted. "In the Chesapeake Bay!"

35   Caroline knew British ships meant one thing—invasion.

36   All over Baltimore church bells clanged, calling militiamen to arms.

37   Men and boys shouldered long muskets and lined up on the parade grounds.

38   A snare drum rolled. A bugle flared. A commander shouted, "Forward, march!"

39   The militiamen tramped off to rout the British.

40   All that day, Caroline tried to go about her work.

41   She sewed.

42   She swept.

43   She looked for her flag and waited for news.

44   She swept and sewed and waited still more.

45   The next day, Caroline heard a low rumble like a distant thunderstorm.

46   Cannon.

47   She whispered a prayer for the men.

48   Later, terrible news was again shouted in the streets. The Americans had fought a battle and lost. Now British troops were headed to destroy Washington.

49   That night, men, women, and children spilled out onto rooftops. They watched the sky over Washington. It glowed an eerie orange. The British were burning the capital!

50   Caroline looked out across the dark harbor toward Fort McHenry. She couldn't see the flag, but she trusted it was there.

51   Baltimore prepared to defend itself.

52   Around the city, men dug trenches and built earthworks. Shovels scraped and clinked. Dirt flew.

53   Women and children carried biscuits and sweet tea to the volunteers.

54   In the channel near Fort McHenry, men sunk small ships and barges to block the harbor.

55   Women and children tore soft cloths into bandages.

56   Men moved gunboats into position, ready to fire on British ships.

57 Once more, Baltimore waited.

58 A day.

59 A week.

60 Two weeks.

61 The city held its breath.

62 And went to church.

63 And went to work.

64 And waited for the British to strike.

65   Early one September morning, a loud roar rocked the flag shop.

66   Caroline rushed to the window.

67   British ships were bombing Fort McHenry!

68   Fort McHenry's guns blazed back!

69   Hour after hour, bombs burst louder than thunder.

70   Hour after hour, rockets screamed and flashed brighter than lightning.

71   The shop trembled and shook. The streets turned thick with smoke.

72   The smell of burnt powder filled the air.

73   The British ships crept closer and closer.

74   Evening came.

75   The sky darkened with storm.

76   Rain fell.

77   Soon thunder and lightning joined the cannon and rockets.

78   Ships and fort and sky boomed and flashed together.

79   Each time the sky lit up, Caroline saw that her flag was still there.

80   At midnight, the bombing stopped.

81   One minute.

82   Ten minutes.

83   An hour, and all was still.

84   Caroline longed for morning light.

85   Now she could only sit.

86   And hold on to courage.

87   She tried not to sleep.

88   But she did.

89   At dawn Caroline awoke. The rain had stopped. Everywhere, sky and water and land looked gray. She couldn't see the fort.

90   A breeze passed through the window. Slowly, the sky cleared.

91   There, hoisted high above the ramparts, Caroline saw a tired flag hanging from its staff in the damp morning air . . .

92   A wool bunting flag sewn full of broad stripes and bright stars.

93   With needles that pricked.

94   And fingers that ached.

95   A flag sewn full of pride and courage and hope.

★   ★   ★

hoisted   If you hoisted a flag, you used ropes to pull it up a pole.

Collaborative Discussion

Look back at what you wrote on page 244. Tell a partner two things you learned. Work with a group to discuss the questions below. Explain your answers by using details from *The Flag Maker*. Take notes and use them to respond.

1 Review pages 246–251. What do the illustrations help you understand about making the flag?

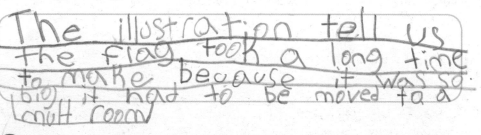

The illustration tell us the flag took a long time to make because it was so big, it had to be moved to a mult room

2 Reread pages 257–259. What details about preparing for the British attack are surprising? Why do you think so?

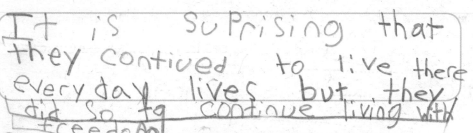

It is suprising that they contived to live there every day lives but they did so to continue living with freedom

3 What details show how Caroline feels about the flag during key events in the selection?

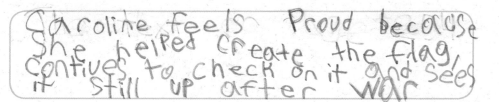

Caroline feels Proud because she helped create the flag, contives to check on it and sees it still up after war

Listening Tip

Listen to the ideas and details each speaker shares. Think about how your ideas can add to, or build on, what they say.

Speaking Tip

Use linking words, such as *another detail* or *also*, to connect your ideas to what other speakers say.

Write a Response

PROMPT

Respond to the Text In *The Flag Maker* you read about Caroline Pickersgill and the story of our nation's flag. What did you learn about the flag and how it was made? How was the flag important in the battle at Fort McHenry? Why is the flag an important symbol to our nation? Cite evidence from the text to support your response.

EVIDENCE

List the ideas from *The Flag Maker* that tell about our nation's flag and why it is important.

Now write your response in a paragraph.

Make sure your response

☐ answers the questions.

☐ uses evidence from the text.

☐ tells about our nation's flag and why it is important.

☐ is written in complete sentences.

Prepare to Read

GENRE STUDY **Narrative nonfiction** gives factual information by telling a story.

- Narrative nonfiction may include headings and subheadings that indicate sections of text.
- Narrative nonfiction may include visuals and text features.
- Narrative nonfiction includes words about the topic.

SET A PURPOSE **Think about** the genre and title of this text. What do you know about the Statue of Liberty? What do you want to learn? Write your ideas below.

The Statue of liberty is a symbol of freedom. I want to know if the torch that she is holding actually has real fier on it.

Meet the Author and Illustrator:
Martha E. H. Rustad and Holli Conger

CRITICAL VOCABULARY

ferry

monument

inspired

torch

sculptor

Why Is the Statue of Liberty Green?

by **Martha E.H. Rustad**

illustrated by **Holli Conger**

A Visit to the Statue of Liberty

1 Our class is going on a field trip!

2 Mrs. Bolt makes us guess where.

3 "What's green and as tall as a twenty-two-story building?" she asks.

4 "A dinosaur!" shouts Elijah.

5 "A green skyscraper!" guesses Elizabeth.

6   "We're going to visit the Statue of Liberty,"
Mrs. Bolt says.

7   "What does liberty mean?" Kiara asks.

8   Mrs. Bolt answers, "Liberty means 'freedom.'"

Statue of Liberty

The Statue of Liberty stands in New York Harbor. Smaller copies of the statue stand in cities around the world, from Paris, France, to Buenos Aires, Argentina, to Fargo, North Dakota.

A symbol is something that stands for something else. The Statue of Liberty stands for freedom.

9   We take a ferry to Liberty Island. We meet Ranger Alisha at the flagpole. She teaches visitors about the monument.

10   "The Statue of Liberty was a gift from France to the United States," she tells us. "It was a symbol of friendship. Workers in France spent nine years building it."

11   "A gift?" asks Ali. "How would you wrap a present that big?"

12   Ranger Alisha says workers took the statue apart and put it in 214 boxes! A ship carried the boxes to New York in 1885.

13   We walk to the front of the Statue of Liberty. The statue sits on a huge base. Ranger Alisha calls it a pedestal.

ferry   A ferry is a boat that takes people or vehicles across a river or waterway.
monument   A monument is a large statue or building that honors an important person or event in history.

The pedestal is 154 feet (47 meters) tall. The statue is 151 feet (46 meters) tall. Together, they are 305 feet (93 meters) tall. That is about as long as a football field!

14   We learn that American workers built the base. "A woman named Emma Lazarus wrote a poem about the Statue of Liberty," Ranger Alisha says. "Her poem inspired thousands of Americans to donate money to buy the pedestal."

15   Then workers put the statue back together on the base. The Statue of Liberty opened to visitors in 1886.

inspired   If an idea or action inspired you, it made you want to do something.

Inside the Pedestal

16 Next, we go inside the pedestal. It's like a museum.

17 "Oh, no!" says Ella. "Did the torch fall down?"

18 Ranger Alisha says this is the old torch. Workers put up a new torch.

torch A torch is a long stick with a flame at one end that may be used for light or to start a fire.

At night, the flame can be seen out at sea from as far as 12 miles (19 kilometers) away.

The green layer is called a patina. It forms when copper mixes with water and changes into a mineral called malachite.

19   She says the new flame is covered in real gold. Lights reflect off the shiny surface.

20   We look at a copy of the statue's face.

21   The nose is taller than we are!

22   "The statue of Liberty is made of copper, like a penny," Ranger Alisha tells us.

23   "But pennies are brown," says Maria. "The statue looks green."

24   "Right!" says Ranger Alisha. "The statue was coppery brown when it was new. Rain, wind, and the sun slowly changed the color to green."

The Big Climb

25   Time to go up the stairs! We climb up 156 steps to the top of the pedestal. "My legs are so tired!" says Tony.

26   We look up—way up—inside the statue. "You can see the steel frame," points out Ranger Alisha. "The frame is kind of like Lady Liberty's bones. It holds her up."

27   Let's go outside!

Sculptor Frédéric-Auguste Bartholdi designed the statue. A man named Gustave Eiffel built the frame. He is famous for building the Eiffel Tower in Paris.

sculptor   A sculptor is an artist who uses stone, wood, or metal to make a work of art.

The statue's full name is Liberty Enlightening the World. People also call it Lady Liberty.

28   "I can see New York City!"
Michael shouts.

29   Ranger Alisha points out Ellis Island.
People who sailed to the United States used
to stop there first when they arrived. These
new Americans sailed past the statue on
their way. "It was the one of the first things
they saw," she says. "She seemed to be
welcoming them to their new home."

About 3.5 million people visit the Statue of Liberty every year.

JULY
IV
MDCCLXXVI

30   "Can we go up to the crown?" Markus asks.

31   "Not this time," says Mrs. Bolt. "Visitors to the crown need special tickets."

32   Andrea says, "My cousin went up to the crown. She said she was as high as the clouds!"

33   Ranger Alisha says there are 377 spiral steps up. And down again!

34   We climb back down the steps. Our field trip is almost done.

35   "What do we tell Ranger Alisha?"
Mrs. Bolt asks.

36   "Thank you, Ranger Alisha!" we shout.

37   As we sail away, Mrs. Bolt says, "The Statue of Liberty is a symbol of freedom. What does freedom mean to you?"

38   "Going to the park without my brother!" says Sarah.

39   "Eating whatever kind of ice cream I want!" Tim says.

40   On the way home, we stop for ice cream. We hold up our cones, just like Lady Liberty's torch!

The Statue of Liberty holds a tablet that reads
July
IV
MDCCLXXVI
This means July 4, 1776, the date of American independence.

Turn Pennies Green

41   **The Statue of Liberty is made of copper. When it was new, it was the color of a penny. Weather caused its green layer to form over time. You can change pennies to match the Statue of Liberty.**

42   **What You Need:**

glass or plastic bowl
1/2 cup vinegar
2 teaspoons salt
plastic or wooden spoon
several pennies
paper towels

43   **1)** Mix the vinegar and salt in a bowl with the spoon.

2) Put the pennies in the bowl. Let them sit for ten minutes.

3) Use the spoon to take out the pennies. Place them on a paper towel to dry.

4) Check the pennies after an hour.

44   **The green layer that forms on the pennies is called a patina.**

Collaborative Discussion

Look back at what you wrote on page 268. Tell a partner two things you learned from this text. Then work with a group to discuss the questions below. Refer to facts and details from *Why Is the Statue of Liberty Green?* Take notes for your responses and use them when you speak. During your discussion, be ready to ask group members questions to help you understand their ideas.

1. Review pages 272–273. How is the Statue of Liberty like a gift you might receive? How is it different?

2. Reread pages 276–277. What details help to explain why people can see the Statue of Liberty from far away?

> People can see it from far away because the monument is very she is green

3. What details in the text explain why the Statue of Liberty is an important symbol for our country?

> It is important because it psybolises are freedom

Listening Tip

Look at each speaker and listen closely. Decide if you agree, disagree, or need to know more to understand the speaker's ideas.

Speaking Tip

If you would like more information, ask a question such as, *Can you help me understand why you said…?*

Write a Response

Respond to the Text In *Why Is the Statue of Liberty Green?*, you read about a well-known national statue. What interesting features does the statue have? What makes the statue special? Why is the statue a symbol of our nation? Cite evidence from the text to support your response.

EVIDENCE

List details from *Why Is the Statue of Liberty Green?* that describe what makes the statue special and why it is a symbol of our nation.

WRITE

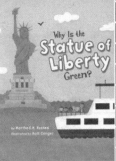

Now write your response in a paragraph.

Make sure your response

☐ uses evidence from the text to answer the questions.

☐ tells why the statue is special.

☐ explains why the statue is a symbol of our nation.

☐ is written in complete sentences.

? Essential Question

How do historic places, documents, and symbols represent our nation?

Write an Expository Essay

PROMPT Think of the people, places, holidays, documents, and symbols that you learned about in this module. Each of these things means something, such as freedom, liberty, or independence, to our nation. Choose three things you read about. Write an expository essay that tells about each one, what it means to our nation, and why. Use evidence from the module selections to support your informative essay.

✓ **Make sure your expository essay**

☐ introduces the topic.

☐ tells about three things you read about in this module.

☐ tells what each thing means to our nation and why.

☐ includes text evidence and examples from the selections.

☐ provides a clear ending statement or conclusion.

Think about the selections in this module. In what ways do the different people, places, things, or symbols mean something to our nation? Choose three examples. Explain what each example means to our nation and why. Use the map below to plan your writing.

My topic: _____

Examples

Detail	Detail	Detail

DRAFT .... Write your expository essay.

Use the information you wrote on page 287 to draft your expository essay.
Write a beginning paragraph that introduces your topic and examples.

Write middle paragraphs that include details about each example. Use
text evidence to support your ideas.

Write a conclusion that summarizes your topic.

The revising and editing steps give you a chance to look carefully at your writing and make changes. Work with a partner to determine whether you have described your topic clearly. Use the questions below to help you.

✓ PURPOSE/ FOCUS	ORGANIZATION	EVIDENCE/ SUPPORT	ELABORATION	CONVENTIONS
☐ Does my essay answer the questions? ☐ Do I clearly explain my ideas about each example?	☐ Do I clearly introduce my topic? ☐ Does my conclusion summarize my topic?	☐ Do I support my ideas with text evidence? ☐ Where do I need to add more evidence?	☐ Do I use linking words to connect ideas? ☐ Do I use words related to my topic?	☐ Have I used capitalization and punctuation correctly? ☐ Have I indented each paragraph? ☐ Have I spelled all words correctly?

PUBLISH .... Create a finished copy.

Make a final copy of your expository essay. Use your cursive writing skills.

Stories on Stage

"The play is not in the words.
It's behind the words."

—Stella Adler

? **Essential Question**

Why might some stories be better told as plays?

Get Curious
Video

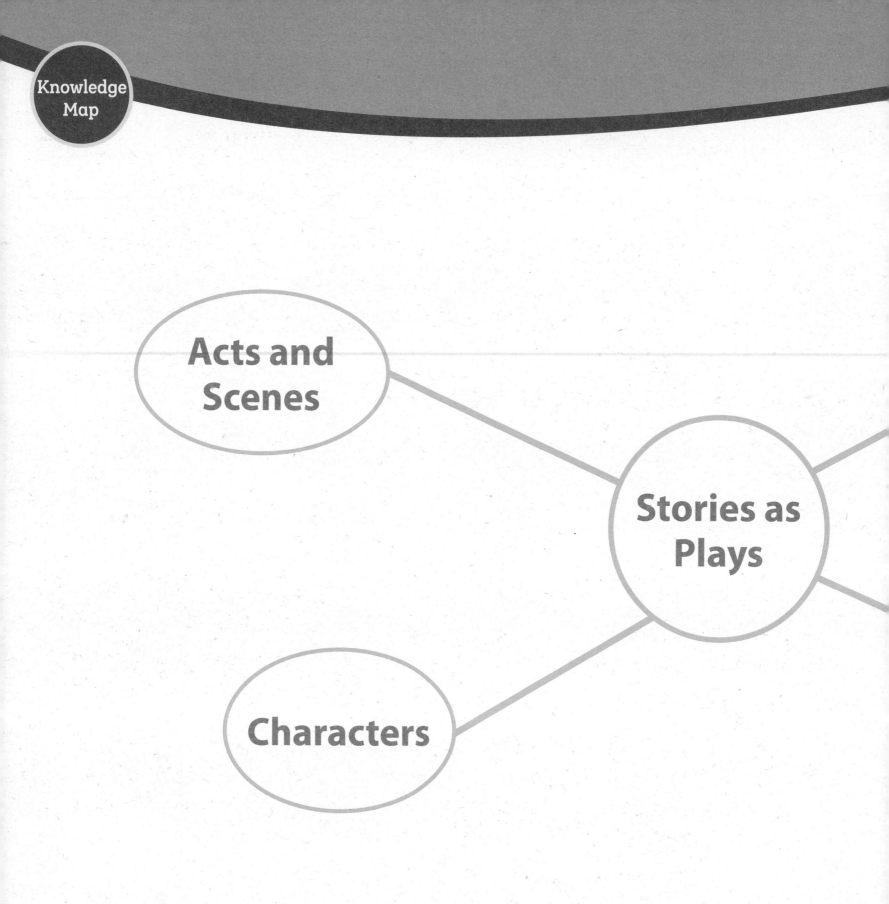

Acts and Scenes

Stories as Plays

Characters

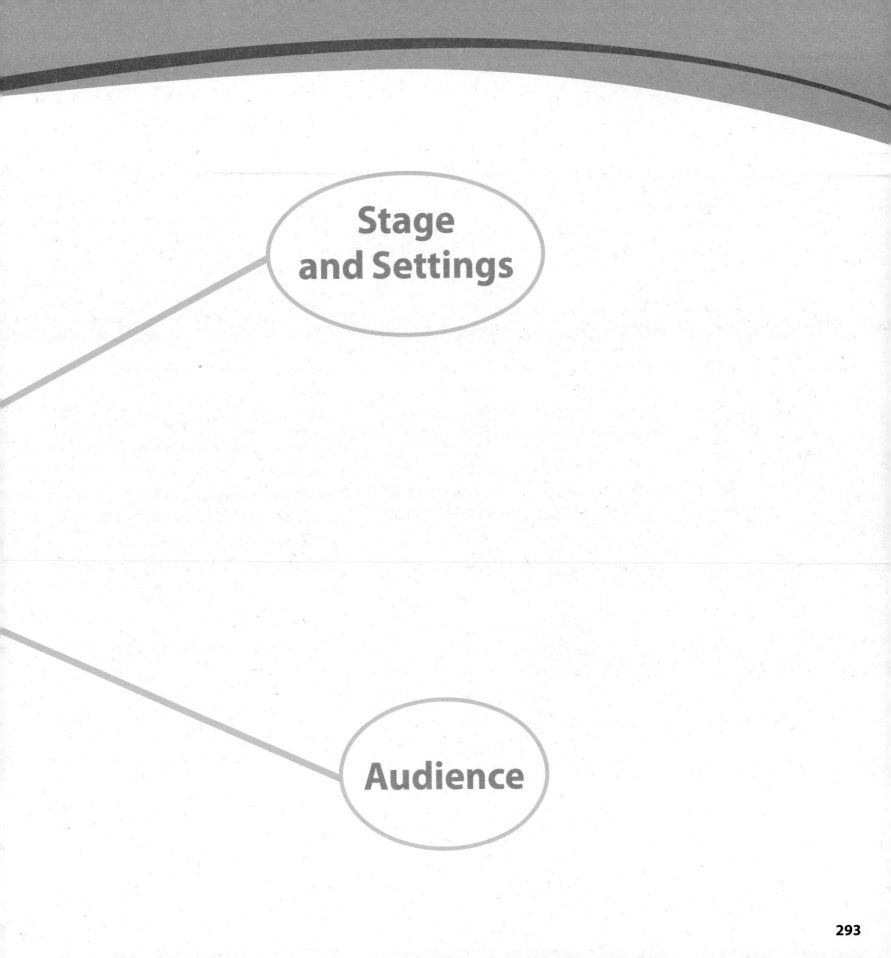

Stage and Settings

Audience

myNotes

THAT'S ENTERTAINMENT!

1   Anyone who has seen a great play will agree: theater is one of the most exciting forms of entertainment. Nothing beats watching skilled actors bringing a story to life on the stage.

2   At the audition, each actor must work hard to win a part as one of the characters. Then it's time to rehearse. The actors take weeks to learn their roles. They read the script and practice their dialogue, or the words they speak on stage. They follow stage directions, which tell actors how to behave and move.

3   Meanwhile, the crew builds sets for the stage to show the play's different settings. The sets include props such as furniture or painted scenery. Each act or scene is like a chapter in a story and may require a different set. Costume designers decide what the actors should wear. The director oversees everything.

4   The play *Peter Pan* is theater at its best. A great script, exciting roles, and colorful stage sets—this play has it all! Written by J. M. Barrie, the play was first performed in 1904. Today, it's as popular as ever. Barrie mixes fantasy and reality to tell an irresistible story. The main character is a boy who never

grows up. Oh, and he can fly! Peter has adventures on the island of Neverland. Mermaids, fairies, and other fantasy characters live there, too. Peter also meets regular children. Unlike Peter, these kids *do* grow up.

5   The play allows set designers to create amazing scenery. There's a towering ship for Neverland's pirate, Captain Hook. Peter's home looks like a fairy tale come to life. *Peter Pan*'s costume designers create fearsome pirate costumes. They make sparkly fairy outfits, too. Both Peter and Tinker Bell, a fairy who is Peter's best friend, "fly" across the stage. How? The crew uses wires and a harness. The audience is in awe!

6   *Peter Pan* offers great parts for actors, too. The starring role of Peter Pan requires an actor who can show a range of emotions. He or she can't be afraid of heights! Captain Hook must be both funny and evil. Wendy, a girl who becomes Peter's friend, must be warm and likable.

7   *Peter Pan* needs a talented director, too. The director must make the set changes go smoothly. The director also needs the ability to coach actors and make them sparkle.

8   Put all these elements together, and you have a thrilling evening at the theater. Entertainment doesn't get better than *Peter Pan*!

Notice & Note
Contrasts and
Contradictions

Prepare to Read

GENRE STUDY A **drama**, or **play**, is a story that can be performed for an audience.

- Plays begin with a cast of characters.
- Authors of plays tell the story through the plot.
- Authors of plays often tell the story in chronological order, or the order in which the events happened.
- Plays are made up of lines of dialogue.

SET A PURPOSE **Think about** the title and genre of this text. This play is based on a tall tale about Pecos Bill. What do you know about tall tales? What would you like to learn? Write your response below.

CRITICAL VOCABULARY

genuine
saga
coiled
whirled
tame

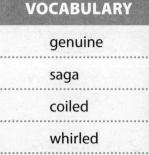

**Build Background:
The Characteristics of Tall Tales**

The SAGA of ★ PECOS BILL ★

written by **Anthony D. Fredericks**
illustrated by **Cory Godbey**

1 **STAGING:** The four narrators should all be seated on stools or high chairs. They should each have their scripts on a music stand or lectern. The other characters (some of whom only have a few lines) may be standing or walking around the staging area.

CHARACTERS:

2

Narrator 1	Pa	Mountain Lion
Narrator 2	Ma	Cowboy 2
Narrator 3	Cowboy 1	
Narrator 4	Pecos Bill	

3 **NARRATOR 1:** Now as you all know, Texas is a pretty big state. In fact, it's the biggest state of them all. And 'cause it's such a big state, it has big heroes. And the biggest of all the heroes was Pecos Bill, the King of the Cowboys.

4 **NARRATOR 2:** You see, Pecos Bill wasn't originally from Texas. No sir. He was from somewhere back east. From a family of 15 or 20 kids. In fact, there were so many kids in the family that the parents just didn't remember all the names of all the children.

5 **NARRATOR 3:** Well, as I heard it, Bill wanted a teddy bear—just like any other kid. But 'cause his family was so poor they couldn't afford a teddy bear just for Bill. So he decided to go out and get his own. So one day he crawled out of his crib and into the woods. There he found a genuine grizzly bear, which he wrapped up in his arms and took on home. Seems like Bill was going to be a little different from everyone else.

> **genuine** If something is genuine, it is real and exactly what it seems to be.

NARRATOR 4: Our saga begins when one day Bill's parents heard about some new land in the West. They heard that there was plenty of land . . . plenty of land for families with 15 or 20 children.

PA: Hey, Ma, I hear that there's plenty of land in the West for families with lots of children.

MA: You mean families like ours with so many children that we just can't remember their names?

PA: Yup!

MA: Well, why don't we just up and move out to that there West so we can build us a house big enough for all these children?

PA: Sounds like a grand idea!

NARRATOR 1: And so Pa and Ma packed all their children and all their animals in the back of their wagon and headed out for the West.

NARRATOR 2: However, as soon as the wagon went over the state line between Arkansas and Texas, it bounced Bill clean out of the wagon and alongside the road.

> **saga** A saga is a long, detailed story about heroic events.

14 **NARRATOR 3:** Since there were so many children and animals in the wagon, nobody noticed that Bill wasn't in the wagon until about a week later. By then it was too late to go look for him, but Bill's parents figured that any baby who could wrestle a grizzly bear was certainly tough enough to survive in the wilds of Texas.

15 **NARRATOR 4:** As it happens, Bill got along fine. After falling out of the wagon, he crawled into a cave of coyotes and fell asleep. The mama coyote took a liking to Bill and began to raise him as her own. Bill soon learned all the ways of coyote life. He learned how to bay at the moon, how to hunt for rabbits, and how to wrestle with all the other coyotes in the den. Pretty soon, Bill was just a regular coyote.

16 **NARRATOR 1:** One day Bill was lapping up some water from the Pecos River along with the other coyotes. That's when a cowboy spotted him.

17 **COWBOY 1:** What in tarnation! You're just lapping up water like you was a regular coyote.

18 **PECOS BILL:** Well, that's what I am—a coyote. Anyways, ain't you never seen a real coyote afore?

19 **COWBOY 1:** 'Course I have. But you're not like any coyote I've ever seen. You look more like a human than you do a coyote.

20 **PECOS BILL:** But I am a coyote. I have fleas just like a coyote, don't I?

21 **COWBOY 1:** That don't mean nothin'. The thing that all coyotes got is a tail.

22 **NARRATOR 2:** With that, Bill turned around and looked back. It was then, for the first time in his life, that he realized he didn't have a tail.

23 **PECOS BILL:** I don't have a tail like my brothers and sisters. But if I'm not a coyote, then what am I?

24 **COWBOY 1:** You're a human being.

25 **NARRATOR 3:** Pecos Bill began to growl just like his coyote mother had taught him. But he knew deep down in his heart that he wasn't a real coyote. So he figured he might as well go along with the cowboy and begin acting like a real human acts.

26 **NARRATOR 4:** Bill started walking alongside the cowboy. Suddenly, a huge mountain lion jumped down from a cliff and right onto Bill's back. Without a thought, Bill just up and wrestled that mountain lion to the ground.

27 **MOUNTAIN LION:** I give up! I give up!

28 **PECOS BILL:** Your huntin' days are over. Seeing as how I need to be more like a human, I'll use you like a horse.

29 **MOUNTAIN LION:** A horse!

30 **PECOS BILL:** Yep, a horse! So let's be on our way.

31 **NARRATOR 1:** Bill jumped on the back of the mountain lion, and he and the cowboy continued on their way.

32 **NARRATOR 2:** They hadn't gone but 10 miles when a 10-foot rattlesnake swung out of a cactus plant and down on top of them.

33 **NARRATOR 3:** Bill jumped off the mountain lion's back and grabbed the end of that snake. He swung that snake around and around his head. As the snake was spinning round and round, it grew thinner and thinner. It also got longer and longer. By the time Bill was done, that 10-foot rattlesnake was 30 feet long.

34 **NARRATOR 4:** Bill coiled up that 30-foot snake just like it was a rope and slung it over his shoulder. From then on cowboys always carried a rope with them just like Pecos Bill carried a 30-foot snake with him wherever he went.

> **coiled** If you coiled something, you shaped it into loops or rings.

NARRATOR 1: After that, Bill and the cowboy rode on until they got to the ranch alongside the Pecos River. The other cowboys didn't know what to make of Bill, riding his mountain lion and carrying a snake wrapped across his shoulders. But I guess they could see that he was a good man, so they figured he'd be a good cowboy, too.

PECOS BILL: Howdy, folks, I'm new in these here parts. I just want to learn how to be a cowboy and help you fellas out.

COWBOY 2: Well, friend, you're welcome to stay as long as you want. We're always looking for new help, seeing as we have the whole state of Texas to take care of and lots of cattle to keep an eye on.

PECOS BILL: I appreciate that. By the way, what would you like to have me do now?

COWBOY 2: Well, I don't think it's anything you can help us with. See, we're just in the biggest drought that Texas ever had. We ain't had no water for months and months now.

40 **PECOS BILL:** Well, I reckon I can help with that.

41 **NARRATOR 2:** And with that, Bill just swung his rattlesnake lasso round and round and he roped up all the water from the Rio Grande River. After that there was no more problem with any drought.

42 **NARRATOR 3:** Seems like there was nothing that Bill couldn't do. Like that time when the biggest and meanest tornado that ever was came into Texas. Bill decided that the only way to tame that tornado was to ride it until it spun itself out.

43 **NARRATOR 4:** So Bill just waited until that tornado came up and over the state line with Oklahoma. It slowed down a little as it crossed into Texas, and that's when Bill just up and jumped on that tornado's back.

44 **NARRATOR 1:** Now, that tornado didn't like anybody ridin' its back. It turned itself from green to brown to black and began to leaping around like it was full of about a hundred wildcats. That tornado whipped and whirled and whipped and whirled some more, just tryin' to throw Bill off its back.

45 **PECOS BILL:** Yowee! Hold on tight! I aim to tame you, seein' as how I'm the toughest cowboy in these here parts. You ain't about to throw me. No sir.

> **whirled** If something whirled, it spun and turned very quickly.
> **tame** If you tame a wild animal, you teach it to do what you want.

NARRATOR 2: Well, that tornado started to do all kinds of mean things as it spun faster and faster. It humped its back, it threw itself all about, it jumped up and it jumped down, trying to toss Bill back on to the ground. It just got meaner and meaner every way it twisted and turned.

NARRATOR 3: In fact, it got to be so mean and so ornery that it tied up rivers into knots and emptied lakes of all their water. Why, Bill and that twister went from one end of Texas to the other—the twister was twisting and Bill was hangin' on for dear life. But try as it might that twister could never throw Bill. No way! Bill just rode that tornado like it was the meanest bull at a rodeo. He jabbed it with his spurs and wrapped his arms tighter and tighter around that spinning tornado.

NARRATOR 4: Finally, that tornado figured it wasn't going to get Bill off its back. So it headed itself out to California and just rained itself out. Seems it rained so much water that it washed out the Grand Canyon. Why, that mean old tornado was worn down to nothing, and by the time they both reached the Pacific Ocean, that tornado was nothing but a little bitty puff of wind.

49 **NARRATOR 1**: When Bill fell off, he hit the ground so hard that the ground just sank right below sea level. Folks in those parts now call that part of California Death Valley.

50 **PECOS BILL**: There, that should teach those tornadoes a thing or two!

51 **NARRATOR 2**: When Bill got back to Texas, he started to clean up the mess he and that tornado made.

52 **NARRATOR 3**: When he first climbed on the back of the tornado, Texas had been covered by forests of trees. But now all the land had been swept clean of every single tree from the full force of that wrestling match between Bill and the tornado.

53 **NARRATOR 4**: And if you go and visit Texas today, you will see lots of wide open spaces all over the state. Wide open spaces thanks to that wrestling match between the greatest cowboy who ever lived and one mean and wild tornado. Yup, Pecos Bill was the best cowboy there ever was . . . the meanest, the strongest, and the best there ever was!

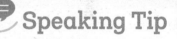

Collaborative Discussion

Look back at what you wrote on page 296. Tell a partner what you learned about tall tales. Then work with a group to discuss the questions below. Use details in *The Saga of Pecos Bill* to explain your answers. Take notes for your responses.

1 Review pages 298–299. What details do the narrators share to show that Pecos Bill was "a little different"?

2 Reread pages 304–305. What words and phrases make it seem like the tornado is a living thing?

3 What did Pecos Bill do that a real person could do? What did he do that a real person could not do?

Listening Tip

Listen closely when others are speaking. Show that you are paying attention by looking at the speaker.

Speaking Tip

Speak clearly and in a way that your group can hear. Be sure that you stay on the topic your group is discussing.

Write a Response

Respond to the Text You have learned that authors of plays tell the stories through the action in the plot, the dialogue of the characters, and the use of a narrator. In *The Saga of Pecos Bill*, you read about Pecos Bill, the larger-than-life hero of this tall tale. What do you learn about Pecos Bill from the narrators? How do the narrators' descriptions help you understand the plot of the play? Cite evidence from the text to support your response.

List details from the narrators in *The Saga of Pecos Bill* that describe Pecos Bill and help you understand the plot of the play.

WRITE

Now write your response in a paragraph.

✓ Make sure your response

- ☐ uses evidence from the text to answer the questions.
- ☐ describes Pecos Bill.
- ☐ explains how the narrators help explain the plot of the play.
- ☐ is written in complete sentences.

Prepare to View

GENRE STUDY ▸ **Informational videos** present facts and information about a topic in visual and audio form.

- A narrator explains what is happening on the screen.

- Informational videos include words that may be specific to a science or social studies topic.

- Videos may include sound effects or music.

SET A PURPOSE ▸ **As you watch,** use what you have learned about plays to help you understand the video. How is the theater's stage different from a stage in your school? What happens off-stage to help make a play sound real? Write your answers below.

▶ Build Background:
Baroque Theater

CRITICAL VOCABULARY

Baroque

pulleys

backdrop

performance

The Traveling Trio:
Český Krumlov, Czech Republic

As you watch *The Traveling Trio: Český Krumlov, Czech Republic*, notice that the children you see in the video are also its narrators. Why do you think the video has narrators who are about your age? Pay attention to the information each narrator gives. Think about how it connects to what you see in the video. Do the narrators explain ideas clearly? Why or why not?

Listen for the Critical Vocabulary words *Baroque, pulleys, backdrop,* and *performance* for clues to the meaning of each word. Take notes in the space below about how the words were used.

Baroque   The Baroque Period was many years ago. The buildings of that time were very fancy and decorated.
pulleys   Pulleys are wheels wrapped with rope that people can use to lift heavy objects.
backdrop   On a stage, a backdrop is a painted curtain or wall that shows the setting of the scene.
performance   If you sing, dance, or speak in front of a group, you give a performance.

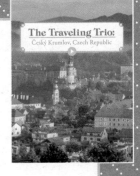

Collaborative Discussion

Work with a group to discuss the questions below. Give examples from *The Traveling Trio: Český Krumlov, Czech Republic* to support your ideas. Take notes for your responses. Be sure to make eye contact with others in your group during the discussion.

1 Why are there very few theaters like the one the children visit?

2 What can you tell about a trapdoor from what the narrator says?

3 What kinds of jobs did stagehands do at the theater?

Listening Tip

Listen to others in your group carefully. Do their ideas agree with yours, or does what they say change what you think?

Speaking Tip

Notice if others seem to understand what you are saying. Do you need to speak more clearly or explain more?

Write a Response

PROMPT ....

Respond to the Video In *The Traveling Trio: Český Krumlov, Czech Republic*, Everett, Olivia, and Ingram took you on a tour of a special theater. What are some of the tools used in an old theater? How do those tools bring a play to life? What do they help the audience understand? Cite evidence from the video to support your response.

EVIDENCE ....

List details from *The Traveling Trio: Český Krumlov, Czech Republic* that help you understand the tools used in old theaters. Note how these tools make plays come to life for the audience.

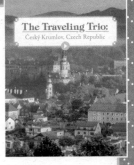

The Traveling Trio:
Český Krumlov, Czech Republic

WRITE

Now write your response in a paragraph.

Make sure your response

☐ uses evidence from the video to answer the questions.

☐ explains how tools are used in old theaters.

☐ tells how these tools make plays come to life.

☐ is written in complete sentences.

Prepare to Read

GENRE STUDY   A **drama**, or **play**, is a story that can be performed for an audience.

- Plays begin with a cast of characters.
- Plays include stage directions and acts or scenes.
- Plays are made up of lines of dialogue with informal language to make the conversation seem real.
- Some plays include a theme, or lesson learned.

SET A PURPOSE   **Think about** the title and genre of this text. This play is based on a classic Italian tale. What do you know about classic tales? What would you like to learn? Write your response below.

CRITICAL VOCABULARY

eminent

peasant

stately

deceive

superior

merciful

**Build Background:
Classic Tales with Magic Rings**

Gigi and the Wishing Ring

adapted from an Italian fairy tale
illustrated by Sumi Collina

Cast of Characters

1

Narrator	Dog
Gigi's Mother	Waiter
Gigi	Three Servants
Old Woman	Maliarda
Cat	Mouse

Setting

2 A small house in a forest. A forest backdrop and a house backdrop with a curtain for a door.

Props

3 A heavy sack, a gold ring, 4 stools, a small table, and a fine cloak

Costumes

4 Human characters wear medieval-style clothes. Animal characters wear animal masks and fur coverings.

ACT I
SCENE 1

5 *(Forest backdrop. Stool at down-right of stage. Lights up full. NARRATOR enters from left and sits on the stool.)*

6 NARRATOR: Once upon a time in Italy, there was a boy named Gigi.

7 *(GIGI enters from left and walks to center stage.)*

8 NARRATOR: Gigi lived in a little house with his mother. One day, though, Gigi decided to go and see the world.

9 *(Offstage)* **GIGI'S MOTHER:** Gigi! Where are you going?

10 *(GIGI'S MOTHER enters from left.)*

11 **GIGI'S MOTHER:** Gigi! Why are you leaving me?

12 **GIGI:** Mama, I want to see the world and seek adventure, and fortune, and stuff.

13 **GIGI'S MOTHER:** Gigi! My heart is breaking!

14 **GIGI:** Don't worry, Mama! It's not like I'm going to get stuck on top of a mountain. That would just be silly! Before you know it, I'll be back with fine clothes and a bag of gold, and we can live happily ever after.

15 **GIGI'S MOTHER:** Oh, Gigi—gold and fine clothes won't make you happy if you don't have a good heart. Do you remember what I told you?

16 **GIGI:** Don't run with scissors?

17 **GIGI'S MOTHER:** No, silly boy! I said that you only *get* from people what you *give* to people!

18 **GIGI:** Sure, sure, Mama, I'll remember. Bye!

19 **GIGI'S MOTHER:** Farewell, my son!

20 *(GIGI'S MOTHER exits left. GIGI marches clockwise around the stage, ending back at center stage. Lights down.)*

SCENE 2

21   *(Lights up. NARRATOR is sitting on the stool down-right. GIGI is standing at center stage and then walks in a circle around the stage.)*

22   **NARRATOR:** Gigi set off to find fortune and adventure and stuff. After many hours, he saw an old woman on the road ahead.

23   *(OLD WOMAN, DOG, and CAT enter from right. OLD WOMAN is carrying a large sack over one shoulder.)*

24   **GIGI:** Hi there! I'm Gigi. Let me carry that heavy sack for you.

25   *(GIGI takes the sack.)*

26   **OLD WOMAN:** Thank you, young man. I thought my back would break.

27   *(GIGI, OLD WOMAN, CAT, and DOG walk slowly to down-left. GIGI sets down the sack.)*

28   **OLD WOMAN:** Your kindness deserves kindness in return. Please, take my cat and dog. Show them loyalty, and they will be your most loyal friends.

29   **GIGI:** Wow, thank you! Hello, Cat.

30   **CAT:** Meow!

31   **GIGI:** Hello, Dog.

32   **DOG:** Woof!

33   **OLD WOMAN:** Take this ring, too.

34   *(The OLD WOMAN hands a gold ring to GIGI.)*

35   **GIGI:** It's beautiful!

36   **OLD WOMAN:** It's not just a beautiful ring. If you ever need something, put the ring on, make a wish, and twist the ring around your finger.

37   **GIGI:** Then what?

38   **OLD WOMAN:** You'll see! One more piece of advice before I go—never, ever tell anyone about your ring. If you do, it will only bring you trouble.

39   *(OLD WOMAN exits left.)*

40   **GIGI:** What a nice old woman! Weird, but nice. OK, guys. Let's go!

41   **CAT:** Meow!

42   **DOG:** Woof!

43   *(GIGI, DOG, and CAT exit right. Lights down.)*

ACT II
SCENE 3

44   *(Lights up. Forest backdrop. NARRATOR is sitting on the stool down-right.)*

45   **NARRATOR:** Gigi and his new friends walked all day. When evening came, they were still deep in the forest.

46   *(GIGI, DOG, CAT enter from left, looking tired.)*

47   **GIGI:** Wow—there sure are a lot of trees in Italy! I need a rest, and something to eat.

48   **CAT** *(sitting down, rubbing its feet)*: Mee-OW!

49   **DOG** *(lying flat)*: Woooof!

50   **GIGI:** I wonder if this ring really works.

51   *(GIGI takes the ring from his pocket and puts it on.)*

52   **GIGI:** OK—I wish for a big bowl of macaroni and cheese . . .

53   **CAT:** Get me a fat tuna, too.

54   **GIGI:** Sure! *(does a double-take)* You can *talk*?!

55   **CAT:** What, you've never met a talking cat before?

56 **GIGI:** No—I can't say I have. Why didn't you say something earlier?

57 **DOG** *(sitting up):* You didn't ask.

58 **GIGI:** You can talk, too?

59 **DOG:** You have a ring that grants wishes. Why are you surprised by talking animals?

60 **GIGI:** Wow—it's like I'm in some sort of fairy tale!

61 **CAT:** Something like that.

62 **DOG:** I'll have a nice, juicy bone, by the way.

63 **GIGI:** OK! I wish for a big bowl of macaroni and cheese, a fat tuna, and a nice juicy bone.

64 *(GIGI twists the ring on his finger. Play slide-whistle sound effect. The WAITER and three SERVANTS enter left and put a table and three stools in center-stage. GIGI, CAT, and DOG sit down. WAITER and SERVANTS exit left. They reenter, set three bowls in front of GIGI, CAT, and DOG and exit left. GIGI, CAT, and DOG pretend to eat from the bowls.)*

65 **GIGI:** Wow, this is tasty!

66 **CAT:** Delicious!

67 **DOG:** Mouth-watering!

68 **NARRATOR:** As the three friends ate their fill, Maliarda, the daughter of an eminent lord, was walking in the forest.

eminent   An eminent person is famous and important.

69 *(MALIARDA enters from the left. She walks to down-left.)*

70 **NARRATOR:** Everyone agreed that Maliarda was the most beautiful girl in Italy.

71 **GIGI:** Wow, she is the most beautiful girl in Italy!

72 *(GIGI stares in awe at MALIARDA.)*

73 **CAT:** Gigi?

74 *(DOG waves hand in front of GIGI's face.)*

75 **CAT** *(loudly):* Gigi!

76 **GIGI:** She's so beautiful! Aw, who am I kidding? A girl like her won't look twice at a peasant like me . . . Wait a minute! I have a wishing ring! I'll wish for fine clothes and a big house and servants. I'll tell her I'm a lord! Then she'll talk to me for sure!

77 **CAT:** Are you sure this is a good idea?

78 **DOG:** It's not nice to lie to people, Gigi.

79 **GIGI:** No, it's OK! I wish for a suit of fine clothes fit for a lord and a big mansion and servants, too.

80 *(GIGI twists the ring around his finger. Play slide-whistle sound effect. The WAITER and three SERVANTS enter from right carrying a fine cloak and the house backdrop. The WAITER puts the cloak around GIGI's shoulders. The SERVANTS place the backdrop upstage center. The WAITER and SERVANTS exit right.)*

81 **GIGI:** That's better! *(To Maliarda)* M'lady!

82 *(GIGI bows deeply.)*

83 **MALIARDA:** Oh, good day to you, sir! Have we met?

84 **GIGI:** No, m'lady. I'm, um, Lord Gigi.

85 **MALIARDA:** It is a pleasure to meet you, my lord. *(To audience)* If he is a lord, I am the Queen of England! *(To GIGI)* Is this your stately home, my lord?

86 **GIGI:** It sure is! Isn't it awesome?

peasant A peasant is someone who is very poor and may work as a farmer.
stately When something is stately, it is awesome or grand.

87 **MALIARDA:** Oh yes, awesome. *(To audience)* How did a peasant like him get such a fine house? I must learn his secret!

88 **GIGI:** What's your name, m'lady?

89 **MALIARDA:** I am Maliarda.

90 **GIGI:** Maliarda! That's a beautiful name!

91 **MALIARDA:** You are too kind, my lord. *(To the audience)* Does this peasant think he can deceive me? Two can play at this game, and I am the superior player! *(To GIGI)* My lord, how did you earn your fortune?

92 **GIGI:** Well . . . it's sort of a secret.

93 **MALIARDA:** Oh I love secrets! I bet it is a really exciting one!

94 **GIGI:** It is!

95 **MALIARDA:** Please tell me!

96 **CAT:** You only just met this girl, Gigi.

97 **DOG:** Yeah, I don't trust her.

98 **MALIARDA** *(shocked)*: How rude! Lord Gigi, are you just going to let your animals insult me like that? Banish them!

deceive   If you deceive others, you tell a lie or try to make them believe something that is not true.

superior   Someone who is superior at something is more skilled than others.

99 **GIGI:** I'm sorry if they offended you, m'lady, but they're my friends. I won't banish them.

100 **MALIARDA:** As you wish, Lord Gigi. Please tell me your secret, though. I promise I won't tell anyone. Please? Pretty please?

101 *(MALIARDA bats her eyelashes at GIGI.)*

102 **GIGI:** Oh, OK! This ring can make wishes come true.

103 **MALIARDA:** That's amazing! How does it work?

104 **GIGI:** You put it on your finger like this.

105 *(GIGI puts the ring on MALIARDA'S finger.)*

106 **DOG:** No, Gigi, don't . . .

107 **GIGI:** Then you make a wish and twist the ring around your finger.

108 **MALIARDA:** I see.

109 *(MALIARDA walks to down-center.)*

110 **MALIARDA:** Well, "Lord" Gigi, I wish that you and your rude friends were on top of the highest mountain in Italy.

111 **GIGI:** What?

112 **DOG, CAT** *(together):* No!

113 *(MALIARDA twists the ring. Play slide-whistle sound effect. Lights out. GIGI, CAT, and DOG exit right. Lights up full again.)*

114 **MALIARDA:** Foolish Gigi, thank you for your wonderful ring and your fine mansion. *(To audience)* If you think I have a cold heart, believe me, it's not as cold as Gigi and his friends are right now.

115 *(MALIARDA exits left, laughing. Lights down.)*

SCENE 4

116 *(Spotlight on NARRATOR on the stool in down-right. Spotlight on GIGI, CAT, and DOG in center stage. They are huddled together. Play howling wind sound effects.)*

117 **NARRATOR:** Gigi and his friends are in big trouble. Thanks to Maliarda, they are on top of the highest mountain in Italy. Freezing winds howl all around them.

118 **GIGI** *(shivering):* S-s-so c-c-c-cold!

119 **DOG:** I can't feel my nose.

120 **CAT:** We have to get out of here!

121 **GIGI:** I don't see any way down. We're trapped!

122 **CAT:** There's no way down on two legs, but I have four! A cat always lands on its feet!

123 **DOG:** Gigi, you've been a good friend. We'll get your ring back from Maliarda.

124 *(CAT and DOG move to down-left, followed by the spotlight. GIGI exits right. Cut the howling wind sound effect.)*

125 **NARRATOR:** Gigi's loyal friends climbed down the mountain. They arrived at Maliarda's house in the middle of the night.

126 *(Lights up full, revealing the house backdrop in upstage center.)*

127 **DOG:** I don't see any lights. Maliarda must be sleeping.

128 *(CAT walks to door and mimes trying to open it.)*

129 **CAT:** It's locked! Now what?

130 **DOG:** I have an idea! I can dig a hole under the door!

131 *(DOG gets on all fours in front of the curtain door and mimes digging. MOUSE enters from left and moves to down-left, watching CAT and DOG.)*

132 **CAT:** You'll need a very big hole.

133 **DOG:** Have you got a better idea?

134 **CAT:** Wait—what's that?

135 *(CAT sees MOUSE.)*

136 **MOUSE:** Eeek!

137 *(CAT chases MOUSE from down-left to stage right. CAT catches MOUSE by the ear.)*

138 **MOUSE:** Ow! Oh, please don't hurt me!

139 **CAT:** Quiet or I'll have you for breakfast!

140 **MOUSE** *(quietly)*: Eeep!

141 **DOG:** This isn't the time for a snack.

142 **CAT:** This is no snack, my friend. This is how we get the ring back. *(To MOUSE)* Listen very carefully. You're going to help us. If you do, we'll let you go. If you don't, it's mouse pancakes for breakfast. Do you understand?

143 **MOUSE** *(nodding)*: Eeep.

144   **CAT:** Squeeze under this door. Inside the house, there's a girl. Find her. There's a gold ring on the girl's finger. Take that ring and bring it to us.

145   **MOUSE:** And then you'll let me go?

146   **DOG** *(standing up):* Yes, little mouse, we'll let you go.

147   **MOUSE:** Oh-oh-OK. I'll help you.

148   *(CAT lets MOUSE go. MOUSE crawls under the curtain door and behind the house backdrop.)*

149   **DOG:** Good thinking, Cat.

150   **CAT:** Thank you, Dog.

151   *(MOUSE crawls back under curtain door.)*

152   **CAT:** Do you have it?

153   **MOUSE:** You wanted me to find a ring?

154   **DOG:** Yes!

155   **MOUSE:** A gold ring?

156   **CAT:** Yes!

157   **MOUSE:** On a girl's finger?

158   **CAT, DOG** *(together):* Yes!

159   **MOUSE:** I didn't find a gold ring on the girl's finger.

160   **DOG:** Oh no!

161   **CAT:** Poor Gigi! How will we save him now?

162   *(MOUSE holds up the ring.)*

163   **MOUSE:** I did find a gold ring on a chain around the girl's neck, but I guess it's not the ring you want.

164   **CAT:** That is the ring we want!

165   **MOUSE:** Oh—that's lucky! Here you go.

166   *(MOUSE hands the ring to CAT.)*

167   **DOG:** Oh, silly mouse, thank you!

168   **MOUSE:** You're welcome, I think. I'll be going then.

169   **CAT:** Good-bye, Mouse. Catch you later!

170   **MOUSE:** Not if I can help it!

171   *(MOUSE exits right.)*

172   **DOG:** Quick, use the ring to save Gigi!

173   *(CAT puts on the ring.)*

174   **CAT:** I wish that Gigi was here right now.

175   *(CAT twists the ring. Play slide-whistle sound effect. GIGI enters from the left.)*

176   **GIGI:** You saved me! Oh, thank you, my friends. Any longer on that mountain and I would have been gelato!

177   *(GIGI, CAT, and DOG high-five.)*

178   **DOG:** I'm so happy to see you, Gigi!

179   **CAT:** Me, too, but what about Maliarda?

180 **GIGI:** I think she deserves a taste of her own medicine. Let me have the ring.

181 *(CAT gives GIGI the GOLD RING. GIGI puts it on his finger.)*

182 **GIGI:** I wish that Maliarda was on top of the highest mountain in Italy.

183 *(GIGI twists the ring. Play slide-whistle sound effect.)*

184 **MALIARDA** *(from offstage):* Oh, noooooo!

185 **DOG:** Gigi, I know she's a terrible person, but it would be cruel to leave Maliarda on top of that mountain.

186 **GIGI:** You're right. I'll be merciful. I wish that Maliarda was only halfway up the highest mountain in Italy.

187 *(GIGI twists the ring. Play slide-whistle sound effect.)*

188 **MALIARDA** *(from offstage):* Not again!

189 **GIGI:** You know, Mama was right. You do get from people what you give to people. I was kind to the old woman, and she was kind to me. I was loyal to my friends, and they were loyal to me. But when I lied to Maliarda, she lied to me.

190 **CAT:** Well, I hope you've learned your lesson, Gigi.

191 **GIGI:** I sure have!

192 **NARRATOR:** Gigi brought his mother to live with him in his new

193 mansion. *(GIGI's MOTHER enters from left and hugs GIGI.)*

194 **NARRATOR:** And they all lived happily ever after.

195 *(Lights out.)*

THE END.

> **merciful** Someone who is merciful is kind and forgiving.

Collaborative Discussion

Look back at what you wrote on page 316. Discuss your response with a partner. Then work with a group to discuss the questions below. Refer to details in *Gigi and the Wishing Ring* to explain your answers. Take notes for your responses.

1 Reread pages 320–321. What do Gigi's words and actions tell you about him?

2 Reread pages 321–323. What parts of the scene could not happen in real life?

3 Review pages 326–329. Which character was most important for saving Gigi—Cat, Dog, or Mouse? Why?

Listening Tip

Listen to the examples each speaker uses. Be ready to explain whether those examples support your own answers.

Speaking Tip

Ask questions if you do not understand what a speaker has said. Point out an exact word or phrase that is not clear to you.

Write a Response

PROMPT

Respond to the Text You learned that the dialogue in a play helps move the plot forward. In *Gigi and the Wishing Ring*, you read about Gigi's search for fortune and adventure. Along the way he meets some interesting characters who teach him important lessons. Think about the interaction between Gigi and the old woman. What does it tell you about these two characters? How does the dialogue between them move the plot forward? Cite evidence from the text to support your response.

EVIDENCE

List details from the dialogue between Gigi and the old woman that help move the plot or action forward.

WRITE ....

Now write your response in a paragraph.

✓	**Make sure your response**
☐	answers the questions.
☐	uses evidence from the text.
☐	explains how dialogue helps readers understand the plot and characters.
☐	is written in complete sentences.

Prepare to Read

GENRE STUDY A **drama**, or **play**, is a story that can be performed for an audience.

- Authors of plays tell the story through the plot—the main events of the story.
- Plays begin with a cast of characters.
- Plays include stage directions.
- Authors of plays might include acts or scenes.
- Some plays include a theme, or lesson learned.

SET A PURPOSE **Think about** the title and genre of this text. This play is based on a Native American myth. What do you know about myths? What would you like to learn? Write your response below.

CRITICAL VOCABULARY

greedily

hesitation

burden

unnoticed

drowsy

reassuring

**Build Background:
The Characteristics of Myths**

TWO BEAR CUBS

retold by Robert D. San Souci

illustrated by Helen Dardik

CHARACTERS

1 **STORYTELLER**
MOTHER GRIZZLY
OLDER BROTHER
YOUNGER BROTHER
HAWK
FOX
BADGER
MOTHER DEER
2 FAWNS
MOUNTAIN LION
MOUSE
MEASURING WORM (*Tu-Tok-A-Na*)

PROLOGUE

2 **STORYTELLER:** (*Enters from stage left*) Many snows have come and gone since this story was first told. My people, the Miwok, live in California—some in what is now called Yosemite Valley. We tell stories of the old days, when animal people lived in the valley. One story begins with MOTHER GRIZZLY going to the river to catch fish for herself and her cubs (*Exits*).

SCENE 1

3 **SETTING:** A forest and mountain, stage left; open sky dotted with clouds, stage right. Blue cloth or painted cardboard across the front of the stage suggests a river.

4 (*MOTHER GRIZZLY enters from stage left, holding a fish basket, and stands on the riverbank. Her cubs, YOUNGER BROTHER and OLDER BROTHER, enter and begin to play in the "water."*)

5 **OLDER BROTHER** (*Laughing and splashing*): Don't be afraid of a little water, Younger Brother!

6 **YOUNGER BROTHER** (*Splashing back*): I'm not, Older Brother!

7 **MOTHER GRIZZLY** (*Scolding*): Children! Stop scaring away the fish, or we will have nothing to eat. Out of the water, now! (*They obey but manage a last splash or two.*) I want you to gather berries—but stay close and do not go downriver. Strange things happen there.

8 (*MOTHER GRIZZLY moves to stage left; the CUBS move to stage right, while playing and pushing each other. A berry bush appears.*)

9 **OLDER BROTHER:** Look at these berries. (*He picks and eats them greedily.*) They are so sweet. Taste them!

10 **YOUNGER BROTHER:** We should take them back to Mother. (*When OLDER BROTHER ignores him, the younger cub begins eating berries, too. Suddenly, he rubs his stomach.*) I have eaten too many!

11 **OLDER BROTHER:** We will bring some back later. Oh, I am full, too.

(*Pointing—*) Let's see what is downriver.

12 **YOUNGER BROTHER** (*Worried*): We are not supposed to go there.

13 **OLDER BROTHER** (*Taunting, starts off*): I see only the river and trees and stones. What is there to fear?

14 (*After a moment's hesitation, YOUNGER BROTHER follows.*)

15 **YOUNGER BROTHER** (*Rubbing his eyes*): I'm tired. The hot sun and my full belly make me want to sleep.

16 **OLDER BROTHER** (*Yawning*): A nap would be good.

---

greedily   When you do something greedily, you take more than you need.

hesitation   A hesitation is a pause that shows you are unsure about doing something.

17 (*A raised platform, decorated to look like a rock, slides into view.*)

18 **YOUNGER BROTHER** (*Pointing*): See that big, flat rock. It looks so warm. Let's rest there. (*The CUBS lie down side-by-side, stretch, and fall asleep.*)

19 **STORYTELLER** (*Entering, stage left*): The cubs fell asleep on the stone. But the stone was the seed of a mountain. As they slept, the stone grew bigger and bigger, higher and higher. (*His hand spiraling upward suggests the growing mountain.*) It carried them so high that only Hawk saw them as he flew by (*Pauses*) . . .

20 (*HAWK enters, stage right, waving his arms like wings. He "flies" past the rock, looks at the sleeping CUBS, and then "flies" back offstage the way he came.*)

21 **STORYTELLER** (*Continuing*): . . . Meanwhile, Mother Grizzly wondered what had become of her cubs. (*Exits stage left*)

SCENE 2

22 (*FOX and BADGER are onstage, leaning cedar planks against a tent-shaped frame of poles.*)

23 **MOTHER GRIZZLY** (*Enters, stage left, calling*): Older Brother! Younger Brother!

24 (*MOTHER GRIZZLY sees FOX and BADGER.*) Fox! Badger! Have you seen my cubs?

25 **FOX:** No. I have been helping Badger build a new home.

26 **BADGER:** Neither of us has seen them. We will help you look for them.

27 (*FOX, BADGER, and MOTHER GRIZZLY search to the right. MOTHER DEER and FAWNS enter, stage left, and seat themselves, grinding acorns. FOX, BADGER, and MOTHER GRIZZLY return to stage left and discover MOTHER DEER and her two FAWNS.*)

28 **MOTHER GRIZZLY:** Mother Deer, my little ones are missing. Have you seen them?

29 **MOTHER DEER:** They have not come by while my children and I were grinding acorns. But we will help you find them.

80 (*MOTHER DEER and FAWNS rise and join the others as they move, to stage right, and then back again, to left. They meet MOUNTAIN LION, carrying a load of firewood.*)

81 **MOTHER GRIZZLY:** Mountain Lion, we are looking for my lost cubs.

82 **MOUNTAIN LION** (*Sets her burden down*): I will help you find them.

83 (*ALL move to stage right, while MOUSE enters from left and sits. MOUSE is weaving a basket. The group at stage right moves left and meets MOUSE.*)

84 **MOTHER GRIZZLY:** Mouse, have you seen my cubs? We have searched everywhere for them. We have looked in hollow logs and caves and in the berry patch and the honey tree.

85 **MOUSE** (*Rising*): No, but I will help you. Perhaps they went downriver.

86 **MOTHER GRIZZLY:** I warned them not to go there.

87 **MOTHER DEER** (*Patting MOTHER GRIZZLY's shoulder and glancing at her own FAWNS*): Sometimes our little ones do not listen very well. I agree that we should look downriver.

88 (*The ANIMALS onstage move slowly toward the "mountain."*)

burden   A burden is something that is heavy to carry.

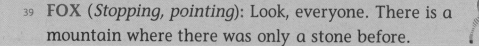

39   **FOX** (*Stopping, pointing*): Look, everyone. There is a mountain where there was only a stone before.

40   (*ALL slowly raise their heads as they scan the mountain from base to summit. As they do, HAWK enters as before, flapping his wings.*)

41   **MOTHER GRIZZLY:** I see Hawk. (*Cups paws around her mouth and shouts "up" to HAWK—*) Hawk! Have you seen my lost cubs?

42   **HAWK** (*Calling "down"*): They are asleep on this strange new mountain.

43   **MOTHER GRIZZLY** (*Calling "up"*): Please fly to my children, wake them, and help them find their way down.

44   (*HAWK pantomimes flying toward CUBS and being blown back by mountain winds. After several tries, he speaks to those "below."*)

45   **HAWK** (*Calling "down"*): The wind will not let me reach your little ones. Someone will have to climb up and rescue them.

46   **STORYTELLER** (*Enters, stage left*): One by one, the animals tried to reach the cubs. (*ANIMALS pantomime their attempts as STORYTELLER speaks.*) Mother Grizzly tried several times but always tumbled back. Mouse jumped from stone to stone but quickly got scared and jumped back down. Badger climbed a bit higher. Mother Deer, a little bit higher. Fox did even better. But none succeeded. Even Mountain Lion failed.

47   (*When MOTHER GRIZZLY sees this, she begins to weep. The other creatures gather around to console her. Unnoticed by them, MEASURING WORM enters.*)

48   **MOTHER GRIZZLY** (*Sadly*): Mountain Lion, you are the best climber and were my best hope. There is no one now who can save my cubs.

49   **MEASURING WORM:** I will try.

50   (*The other animals turn and stare at him, and then ALL except MOTHER GRIZZLY begin to laugh.*)

51   **MOUNTAIN LION:** Foolish Measuring Worm! Do you think you can do what the rest of us have failed to do?

52   **MOUSE** (*Meanly*): *Tu-tok-a-na!* Your name is longer than you are.

53   **STORYTELLER** (*Appearing stage left*): My people call Measuring Worm *Tu-tok-a-na*, which means "Little Curl-Stretch." He moves by stretching—*tu*—then curling—*tok*—the way a caterpillar moves.

unnoticed   When something is unnoticed, it is not seen by anyone.

54 **MOTHER GRIZZLY** (*Drying her eyes*): I welcome your help.

55 (*MEASURING WORM begins to climb, all the while crying, "Tu-tok!" The other ANIMALS sit, staring at the mountain, watching as the WORM stretches and curls in a climbing motion.*)

56 **MEASURING WORM** (*Loudly*): *Tu-tok! Tu-tok!*

SCENE 3

57 **STORYTELLER:** In time Measuring Worm climbed even higher than Mountain Lion. He climbed so high that the animals below could no longer see or hear him. Sometimes he would grow afraid and stop when he saw how high he had climbed and how much higher he had to go. Then he thought about poor Mother Grizzly so worried at the bottom of the mountain. He thought about the cubs in danger at the top. Then he found his courage again and continued to climb, all the while crying—

58 **MEASURING WORM:** *Tu-tok! Tu-tok! Tu-tok!*

59 (*STORYTELLER exits as MEASURING WORM finally crawls onto the rock. He bends over the two sleeping CUBS and calls—*)

60 **MEASURING WORM:** Wake up!

61 (*The CUBS are drowsy as they wake and stretch and yawn.*)

> **drowsy** A drowsy person is sleepy and not able to think clearly.

344

62 **OLDER BROTHER** (*Crawls and looks over the side of the "rock"*): Younger Brother! Something terrible has happened. Look how high we are.

63 **YOUNGER BROTHER** (*Also on his knees, peers down*): We are trapped here. We will never get back to our mother. (*The CUBS begin to cry. They have forgotten MEASURING WORM.*)

64 **MEASURING WORM** (*Comforting the CUBS*): Do not be afraid. I have come to guide you safely down the mountain. Just follow me, and do as I say. We will follow the safe path that brought me here.

65 **OLDER BROTHER:** I am afraid I will fall.

66 **YOUNGER BROTHER:** I am scared, too.

67 **MEASURING WORM** (*Gently*): Surely Mother Grizzly's children are not so afraid, for she is the bravest creature in the valley.

68 **OLDER BROTHER** (*Puffing out his chest, and beating it with his paw*): We are grizzlies. We are brave.

69 **YOUNGER BROTHER** (*Doing the same*): We will follow you.

70 (*They pantomime following a safe path in single file, with MEASURING WORM leading, OLDER BROTHER following, and YOUNGER BROTHER behind. Below, FOX suddenly spots something, stands up, and peers more closely.*)

71 **FOX** (*Excitedly, pointing to a spot about halfway up the mountain*): Mother Grizzly. Look! Measuring Worm is guiding your cubs down the mountain.

72 (*All ANIMALS look where FOX is pointing.*)

73 **MOTHER GRIZZLY** (*Joyful, fearful*): Be careful, my children!

74 **MOTHER DEER** (*Reassuring her friend*): Trust Measuring Worm. He has brought them safely this far. He will not fail you now.

75 (*The ANIMALS continue to watch. They slowly lower their gaze to follow the climbers as they come down the mountain. At last the CUBS and MEASURING WORM make a final leap from the "mountain" to the "ground." The CUBS run to their mother. MOTHER GRIZZLY gives them a big hug. Then she pushes them away and shakes her finger at them.*)

reassuring If you are reassuring a friend, you are trying to keep him from worrying about something.

76 **MOTHER GRIZZLY** (*Scolding*): Both of you have been very naughty! Look at the trouble and worry you have caused us all. You did not listen to me and went where you were not supposed to go!

77 **OLDER BROTHER** (*Hanging head*): I'm sorry. I won't do it again.

78 **YOUNGER BROTHER** (*Starting to cry*): I will never disobey you again.

79 **MOTHER GRIZZLY** (*Gathering them up in her arms again*): Be sure that you remember what happened today. But do not cry, little ones. It has all ended well, thanks to the help and courage of Measuring Worm.

80 (*The ANIMALS gather around MEASURING WORM and congratulate him.*)

81 **STORYTELLER** (*Enters, stage left*): Then all the animals decided to call the new mountain *Tu-tok-a-nu-la*, which means "Measuring Worm Stone." This was to honor the heroic worm who did what no other creature could do—he saved the two bear cubs. The mountain held this name for many years, until newcomers named the mountain El Capitan. We Miwok still call the mountain *Tu-tok-a-nu-la* to this day.

THE END

Collaborative Discussion

Look back at what you wrote on page 334. Discuss your response with a partner. Then work with a group to discuss the questions below. Use details in *Two Bear Cubs* to explain your answers. Take notes for your responses.

1 Review pages 338–339. What details in the play help you know what Older Brother and Younger Brother are like?

2 Reread pages 342–343. Why is it a surprise when Measuring Worm offers to try to save the bear cubs?

3 What does the play show about how the Miwok people thought of animals?

Listening Tip

Listen closely to other speakers. Think about how you can connect your ideas to theirs.

Speaking Tip

Be sure that all of your comments are about the topic your group is discussing.

Write a Response

Respond to the Text You learned that stage directions in a play tell how actors should move and speak. In *Two Bear Cubs*, you read a Miwok myth about several animals who try to help two bear cubs return home safely. How do the stage directions help you better understand the characters? What do you learn about the characters' actions from the stage directions? Cite evidence from the text to support your response.

EVIDENCE

List stage directions from *Two Bears Cubs* that helped you understand the characters and their actions.

WRITE

Now write your response in a paragraph.

✓	Make sure your response
☐	answers the questions.
☐	uses evidence from the text.
☐	explains how the stage directions helped you understand the characters.
☐	is written in complete sentences.

? Essential Question

Why might some stories be better told as plays?

Write an Opinion Essay

PROMPT Think about the plays you read in this module. Review the elements of plays, such as narrator, dialogue, and stage direction. How do these elements help tell the stories? Write an opinion essay about whether or not you think the stories in this module worked well as plays. Use evidence from the module selections to support your opinion.

Make sure your opinion essay
☐ states your opinion clearly.
☐ includes reasons supported by evidence and examples from the selections.
☐ presents your reasons in a logical order.
☐ uses transition words and phrases, such as *because* and *for example*.
☐ sums up your opinion in a conclusion.

Each text in this module is written as a play. Do you think this format was the best way to tell each story? Consider the elements of a play. Could the story be told without these elements? Would it be as good? Use the map below to plan your writing.

Opinion

Reason 1

Reason 2

Reason 3

DRAFT .... Write your opinion essay.

Use the information you wrote on page 353 to draft your opinion essay. Write an introduction that clearly states your opinion about whether or not the stories told in this module work well as plays.

Write a paragraph that includes the reasons and text evidence that support your opinion. Present your reasons in an order that makes sense.

Conclude your essay by restating your opinion.

REVISE AND EDIT .... Review your draft.

The revising and editing steps give you a chance to look carefully at your writing and make changes. Work with a partner to determine whether you have explained your ideas clearly. Use the questions below to help you.

PURPOSE/ FOCUS	ORGANIZATION	EVIDENCE/ SUPPORT	ELABORATION	CONVENTIONS
☐ Does my essay answer the questions? ☐ Do I explain my opinion about the plays in this module?	☐ Do I explain my reasons in an order that makes sense? ☐ Does my conclusion restate my opinion?	☐ Have I included text evidence and examples from the selections?	☐ Have I used transition words to connect my opinion and reasons?	☐ Have I spelled all words correctly? ☐ Have I used correct punctuation and capitalization?

PUBLISH .... Create a finished copy.

Make a final copy of your opinion essay. Use your cursive writing skills.

355

Teamwork

"Talent wins games, but teamwork
and intelligence win championships."
—Michael Jordan

? Essential Question

What can sports teach us about working together?

Get Curious

Video

Skills

Working
Together as
a Team

Supporting
Each Other

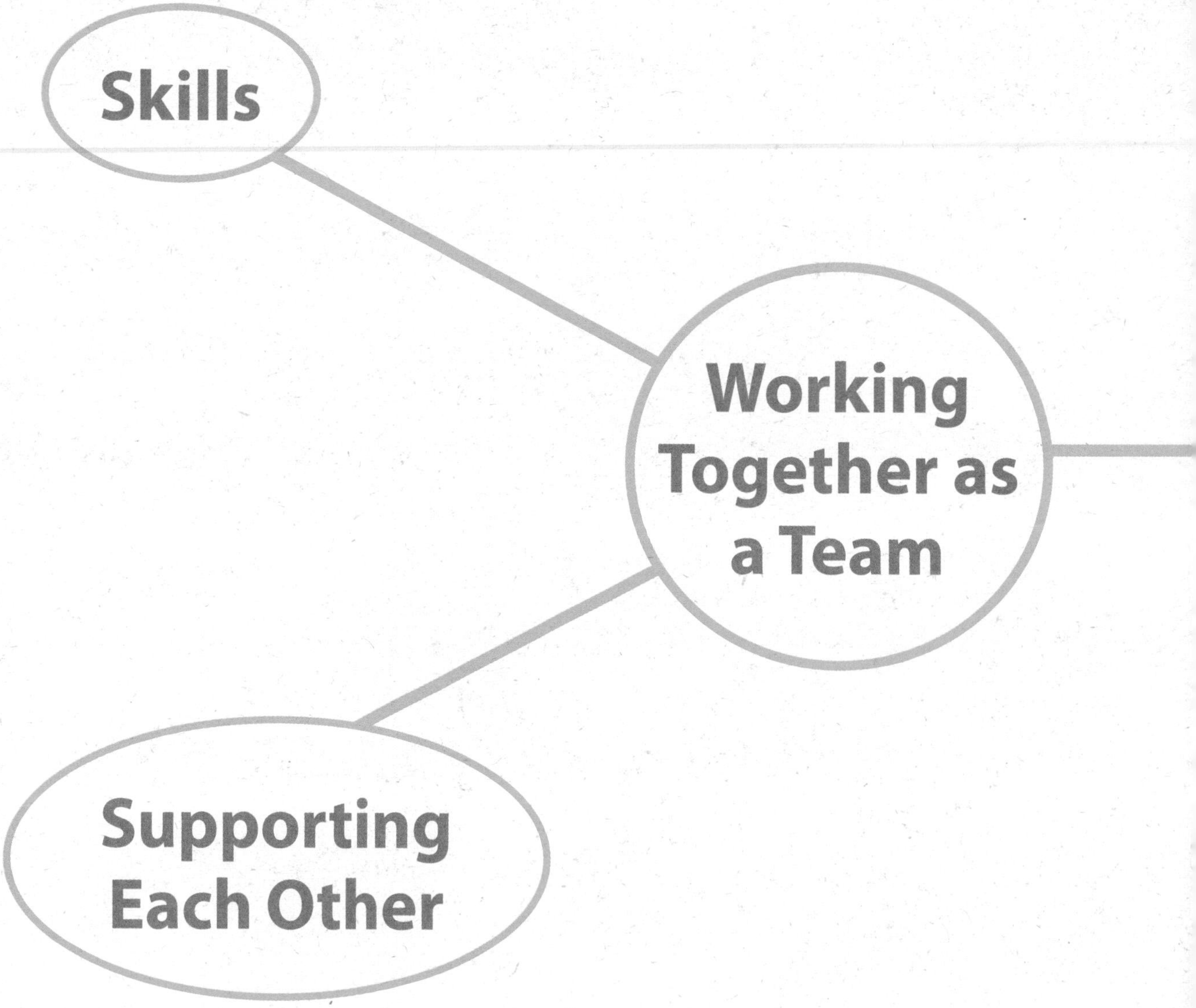

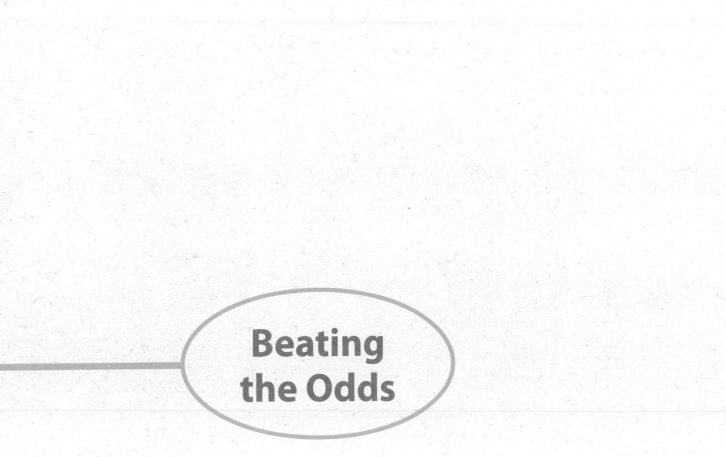

Beating the Odds

collaboration
Collaboration is working together in a group to accomplish a task.

symbiosis
Symbiosis happens when two individuals closely work together and both benefit from it.

unity   Unity is when people join together for a common idea or cause.

determination
When you keep trying until you succeed, you show determination.

myNotes

Short Read

TEAMWORK=VICTORY!

1 Everyone knows teamwork is important in basketball, yet fans often focus on only the star players. Stars are the ones who score all the points. Many fans stand and cheer for only their favorite players. But every player's success depends on the collaboration of the whole team.

2 Those fans might have been surprised last night. The Thompson High School girls basketball team won the state championship, beating Marshland High 65–47. The Thompson Owls don't have any big stars. The Marshland Ravens do. So how did the Owls win? Working together was the key.

3 Sheila Ramirez scored 30 points, making her the Owls' high scorer last night. But Ramirez isn't known for being a high-scoring player. She tends to pass the ball as often as she shoots it. Kate Na of the Owls stole the ball from the Ravens ten times, passing it to Ramirez or to Haley Sears to score. They had an unstoppable symbiosis. Each player helped the others to be their best.

4 No one expected the Owls to outshine their opponents. The Ravens' Yasmin Vergera was the league's highest-scoring player all season. She rarely missed an opportunity to take a shot. Cheyenne Jamison is an ace defensive player. She set the record for stealing the ball this season. She's known for trying to shoot from the far end of the court instead of passing the ball. When she succeeds, fans go wild.

5 But last night wasn't about big stars and flashy moves. "It was all about unity," said the Owls' coach, Malia Stephens. "Playing as a team, not as individuals, got us the win. Well, determination helped, too. Our players never quit!"

6 The Owls fell behind early. Still, they refused to give up. They figured out how to stop Yasmin Vergera from scoring. Their defense was on fire! They also found a way to get around the Ravens' defense with a strong passing game. Look at the Owls' statistics, and you'll see the story.

Player	Points	Rebounds	Steals
Sheila Ramirez	30	6	2
Haley Sears	15	3	0
Kate Na	8	4	10
Lin Littleton	6	1	3
Luisa Okeha	6	2	0
Rachel Healey	3	1	1
Shyla Burdock	2	1	2
Teanna O'Connor	2	1	0

Prepare to Read

GENRE STUDY **Realistic fiction** tells a story about characters and events that are like those in real life.

- Authors of realistic fiction tell the story through the plot—the main events of the story.
- Realistic fiction includes characters who act, think, and speak like real people.
- Realistic fiction includes dialogue and informal language to make the conversations seem real.
- Some realistic fiction includes a theme or lesson.

SET A PURPOSE **Think about** ways an author makes the characters and events seem real. What are some ways that you might relate to the characters in the story? Write your response below.

Meet the Author:
Jake Maddox

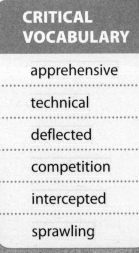

CRITICAL VOCABULARY

apprehensive

technical

deflected

competition

intercepted

sprawling

SOCCER SHOOTOUT

by JAKE MADDOX
illustrated by Matthew Shipley

1 After helping to win their school's first ever state soccer championship against the Cosmos, Peter and Berk are looking forward to another soccer season. At spring tryouts, both boys are working hard to practice their skills. Peter is a star forward. Berk is the goalkeeper who had saved the day in the state championship. Peter tells Berk that he heard there is a new student at school who will also be trying out for goalkeeper. Berk meets the new boy, Ryan, who is very confident. Berk is worried and a little apprehensive going into tryouts.

TRYOUTS

2 It didn't take long for the differences between Berk and Ryan to become clear during tryouts.

3 As they worked on various drills, Berk was clearly better at many of the technical parts of the game.

4 He made good decisions on when to come out of the goal to challenge a shooter or to pick up a loose ball. He always seemed to be in the right place at the right time.

5 When shots were taken on him, Berk made solid saves and controlled the rebounds.

6 Ryan was a little wilder in the goal. He took unnecessary chances, coming out of the net to challenge a player when it would have been smarter to stay back. He often found himself out of place.

apprehensive   If you are apprehensive, you are worried something bad might happen.

technical   The technical parts of a sport are the basic skills and understanding that are needed to play.

7   But Ryan was a better athlete than Berk. So he often covered his own fundamental mistakes by making spectacular diving saves.

8   On the second-to-last day of tryouts, Coach Davis broke the Titans into two teams for a scrimmage.

9   The teams were pretty evenly matched. Berk was in one goal, Ryan was in the other. Peter was on Berk's team.

10   Before the scrimmage, Peter ran up to Berk. "Don't worry, buddy," he said. "I'll score on him and then you'll have the keeper job."

11   At first, the scrimmage was going just as the drills had gone. Berk was always in the right place.

12   When any shots were taken at him, Berk was ready, so the saves were pretty easy to make.

13   Ryan was running all over the field. At one point, he charged a forward who had the ball in the corner. That left the whole goal wide open, so the forward lofted a pass toward Peter.

14   Peter met the pass in the penalty area. He controlled the ball with his left foot, then blasted it with his right toward the open net. But Ryan's quickness allowed him to get back to the net. He dove across to his right and deflected Peter's pass toward the right post.

15   Another forward pulled the rebound in on the right side of the net.

16   Again Ryan charged, and the forward put the ball out front.

17   This time Peter tried to redirect the ball toward the left post. He didn't aim it perfectly, and Ryan dove back on top of the loose ball.

18   Berk's heart sank. He knew that if the same play had happened to him, neither of those shots would have been taken.

19   He would have stopped the first pass, and the play would have been over. But Ryan's wild style allowed him to make two spectacular-looking saves. Even Coach Davis was clapping and yelling.

20   Neither team scored in the scrimmage. Afterward, Coach Davis called Berk over to the sideline. "Berk," he said. "I have an idea."

21   Idea? Berk wasn't sure what to say.

22   Then the coach continued: "Have you ever thought about playing another position?"

deflected   If you deflected something that was moving, you made it go in a different direction.

NEW POSITION?

23   Berk decided to be honest with his coach.

24   "Um, no, Coach," he said. "I've always wanted to be a goalkeeper."

25   Coach Davis put his arm around Berk's shoulder.

26   "Well, you have such great footwork, and you're always in the right place at the right time," Coach Davis said. "I think you might make for a great sweeper."

27   The sweeper plays right in front of the keeper. He is often the keeper's most trusted teammate.

28   The sweeper helps protect the goalkeeper and clears away loose balls in front of the net.

29 It was a very important position, Berk knew. And since Michael Swenson, the boy who played it last season, had moved, the position was open.

30 Still, Berk wasn't interested in it. "I'd rather play keeper," he said.

31 "I know," Coach Davis said. "But I think I'm going to go with Ryan in goal."

32 Berk was shocked.

33 It had been a long time since he'd cried about anything to do with sports, but he felt like it now.

34 "You'll be the backup keeper," Coach Davis continued. "And you'll still play all the time, because you'll be the sweeper."

35 Berk managed to mutter something that sounded like "Okay," but he was still fighting back tears.

36 As the players left the field, he ran off ahead of the group.

37 He changed clothes quickly and got on his bike for the short ride home.

38 One more day of tryouts remained, but Berk already knew where he stood.

39 On the final day of tryouts, he didn't even bring his goalkeeper gloves to the field. He practiced the entire time with the defenders.

40 During a break, Peter ran up to Berk.

41 "What the heck are you doing?" Peter asked. "Why aren't you fighting for the keeper spot?"

42 "Coach told me yesterday," Berk said. He couldn't bear to look at his friend. He kept his eyes fixed on the ground. "I'm going to be sweeper."

43   "That stinks," Peter said. "At least you'll be on the field all the time with me."

44   Berk smiled a little. Just then, Ryan ran over for a drink of water. He walked right up to the boys. Berk cringed as he prepared for Ryan to gloat.

45   "Hey, Berk," Ryan said. "You're a good keeper. I'm sorry tryouts didn't turn out the way you wanted."

46   Berk was sure Ryan didn't mean what he said. "Yeah," Berk said. "Whatever."

47   "It was a good competition," Ryan said. He held out his hand to Berk. "No hard feelings?"

48   Berk shook Ryan's hand for a quick second. "No hard feelings," he forced out. Ryan trotted away.

> **competition**   If you are in a competition, you are in a contest against another person or team.

LET THE GAMES BEGIN

49   After just a few weeks of practice, the Titans were ready to begin their season.

50   It would be a long schedule. There were twenty-four league games, plus four weekend tournaments.

51   "Well, boys, we're ready for another great season," Coach Davis began. "Last year, we won the state tournament. I know some things are different this year, but I think we can do it again. And we have a new opportunity this year. Whoever wins the state title this year will be invited to play in a national tournament!"

52   Now the players were pumped. They couldn't wait to get on the field.

53   When the game began, Berk felt strange. Playing as sweeper meant moving around the field a lot and doing things that he wasn't used to doing.

54   Still, he handled the position well, so Ryan didn't have much work at the net.

55   The Titans controlled play for most of the game.

56   Peter scored a goal late in the first half to give the team a 1–0 lead against their opponents, the Storm.

57   Midway through the half, the Storm pushed the ball down into the left corner of the field. Ryan charged out of the net to challenge the forward. That left the net empty.

58   "Ryan!" Berk yelled. "Get back in the goal!"

59   It was too late.

60   A Storm player hit the ball into the middle of the field.

61   Berk couldn't get to it, and the Storm's center forward pounded the ball into the open net. Ryan dived, but couldn't reach the shot.

A LITTLE HELP

62   The Storm and the Titans ended the game in a 1–1 tie.

63   The rest of the Titans' season was a lot like that first game.

64   Ryan made some great saves, but his poor fundamental play cost his team several goals.

65   The Titans were scoring as many goals as they had the year before, but they were giving up a lot more.

66   After that first game, when Ryan didn't seem to like Berk's advice, Berk stopped giving it. He did his best job as sweeper, trying to protect Ryan. But he didn't offer Ryan any help in how to play goalkeeper.

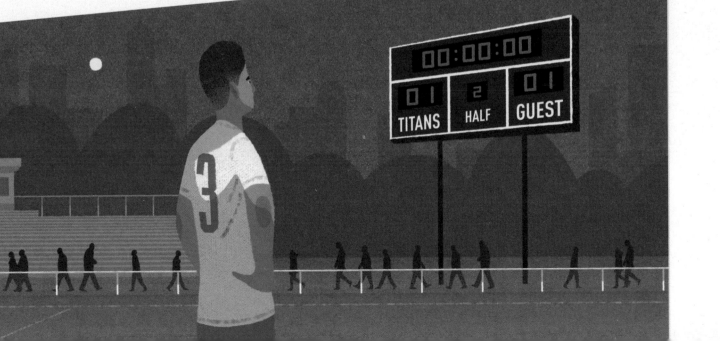

67   The Titans were barely able to make the league playoffs.

68   After the last game of the regular season, Coach Davis took Ryan aside for a private talk. Berk couldn't hear what they were saying.

69   When the talk was over, Coach Davis called to Berk.

70   Berk ran up to him.

71   "Berk, I think we need to make a change," Coach Davis said. "I'd like to put you back in goal for the playoffs."

72   Berk wasn't sure what to say.

73   "Are you sure?" Berk said. "Ryan's been playing there all year."

74   "It's not working out," Coach Davis said. "If we want to go to nationals, we need you in goal."

75   It was a huge compliment, and Berk knew it.

76   Still, he felt uneasy. "Um, thanks, Coach," he finally said.

77   As the coach walked away, Peter approached. "I heard the great news!" he yelled. "That's awesome!"

78   "Yeah, awesome," Berk mumbled. "So why don't I feel better?"

79   That night at home, Berk pulled out his goalkeeper gloves. He tried them on. This time, they felt a little funny.

80   Berk stared at the gloves, and things suddenly became clear.

81   That night, Berk phoned Peter and asked if he could meet at the soccer field.

82   "Trust me," Berk told his friend. "I have an idea."

HELPING OUT

83   Berk walked over to Ryan's house. He rang the doorbell and waited.

84   He wasn't sure how Ryan would react to him coming over. After all, they weren't exactly friends.

85   Ryan came to the door. When he saw Berk, he paused for a moment. Then he opened the door and stepped out.

86   "So, did you come over to gloat?" Ryan said.

87   "Not exactly," Berk said. "I have an idea."

88   Ryan looked confused.

89   Berk didn't worry about what he was about to say.

90   He decided direct honesty was the only way.

91   "Look, you make better saves than I do," Berk said. "But you're not a better goalkeeper than me."

92   "So you did come over to gloat," Ryan shot back.

93   "Just listen," Berk replied. "If we put our skills together, we'd have an awesome goalkeeper. So that's what we need to do."

94   "Huh?" Ryan said. "What are you saying? Are you nuts?"

95   "We need to combine our skills into one keeper," Berk said. "I'll never be able to make some of the amazing saves you make, because you're a better athlete than I'll ever be. But you can learn how to play goalkeeper as well as I do."

96   It was all becoming clear to Ryan. "So, you're going to help me with the fundamentals?" he said.

97   "Exactly," Berk said.

98   Throughout that weekend, Berk and Peter drilled Ryan on the fundamentals.

99   It wasn't easy, but Ryan was starting to get it.

100   At the next practice, Berk and Ryan approached Coach Davis together.

101   They presented their idea, and told the coach what they had already done.

102   Coach Davis seemed pleased.

103   "I'm not sure if this will work," he said. "But I'm proud of you boys for working together to solve this problem. Let's do it!"

PLAN IN ACTION

104   It wasn't always smooth, but the plan worked.

105   Berk shouted "Goal!" whenever Ryan needed to stay put, and "Now!" when he needed to charge.

106   After a few games, Berk didn't need to make the calls anymore.

107   Ryan was figuring it out on his own.

108   Ryan kept making spectacular saves.

109   The Titans easily advanced through the league playoffs and the first two rounds of the state tournament.

110   In the state championship, they again faced the Cosmos, just as they had the year before. This was it, their chance to go to nationals for the first time ever.

111   Early in the second half, Berk intercepted a pass at the top of the penalty area.

112   Looking ahead, he heard Peter yell "Send it!" as he took off down the sideline. Berk booted the ball high down the field, ahead of Peter.

113   With his speed, Peter beat the defense and controlled the pass.

114   He closed on the Cosmos goal and boomed a heavy shot toward the far upper corner.

intercepted   If you intercepted something, you stopped it from getting where it was going.

115   As the ball hit the webbing of the net, Berk and the rest of the Titans yelled.

116   They were ahead!

117   Now they only needed to protect their lead. Against the Cosmos, it wasn't going to be easy.

118   In the final minute, the Cosmos made one last rush up the field. They moved the ball into the corner, and a Titans defender rushed to challenge.

119   Berk moved to cover a player. But with the game on the line, the Cosmos brought more players into the zone.

120   The Titans defenders couldn't cover them all.

121   The Cosmos player kicked the ball toward the front of the goal.

122   Ryan froze. Berk could tell he was trying to decide if he should run out to try to play it or if he should stay in the goal.

123   Ryan stayed put. He saw the ball going toward an unguarded player near the penalty-kick dot.

124   Ryan prepared for the shot. He crouched low and kept his hands ready.

125   When the ball bounced off the player's foot, Ryan was ahead of it.

126   His sprawling dive met the ball perfectly. And, instead of knocking it away, Ryan caught it. He clutched it tightly as time expired.

> **sprawling**   If you move in a sprawling way, you spread out your arms and legs.

127   The Titans were champions again!

128   Peter and Berk rushed to their keeper. Ryan still held the ball to his chest.

129   "You did it!" Berk yelled. "You did it!"

130   Ryan looked him in the eye. "No, we did it," Ryan said.

Collaborative Discussion

Look back at what you wrote on page 362. Discuss your response with a partner. Then work with a group to discuss the questions below. Refer to details in *Soccer Shootout* and take notes for your responses. As you discuss, keep good eye contact and make sure each person gets a chance to speak.

1 Reread pages 364–365. In what ways is Ryan different from Berk as a goalkeeper?

>

2 Review pages 367–368. What words and actions show how Berk feels about being the sweeper on the team?

>

3 How does the way Berk and Ryan think of each other change by the end of the story?

>

Listening Tip

Listen for reasons speakers give when answering a question. What questions could you ask to help them explain more about their ideas?

Speaking Tip

Think about the questions speakers ask. In your answer, include specific details from the selection that will help you explain what you think.

Write a Response

PROMPT

Respond to the Text In *Soccer Shootout*, you read about two soccer players who must work together to make their team better. Although Berk and Ryan are on the same team, they are competing against each other. Why? How do they overcome this challenge? What happens when they work together? Cite evidence from the text to support your response.

EVIDENCE

List details and ideas from *Soccer Shootout* that tell what happens when Berk and Ryan work together. Note what they learn from that experience.

Now write your response in a paragraph.

✓ Make sure your response

☐ uses evidence from the text to answer the questions.
☐ explains how the boys overcame their challenges.
☐ tells what the boys learn from working together.
☐ is written in complete sentences.

Prepare to View

GENRE STUDY ▶ A **humorous fiction video** tells an entertaining story in visual and audio form.

- The purpose of a humorous fiction video is to tell a story that makes the viewer laugh.
- Humorous fiction videos might use real people and places to tell the story with or without animation.
- Sound effects or music may be added for interest.

SET A PURPOSE ▶ **As you watch,** recall what you know about story elements to help you understand the characters and the plot in the video. How does the video create humor? What makes Bianca different from the other members of the team? Write your answers below.

CRITICAL VOCABULARY

captain

force

finals

**Build Background:
The Idiom "Bend It like . . ."**

Bend It Like Bianca

As you watch *Bend It Like Bianca*, notice the visuals and sounds that are used. How do the visuals and sounds make the video humorous or entertaining? Do the visuals and sounds help you understand the story better? Why or why not? Take notes in the space below.

Listen for the Critical Vocabulary words *captain*, *force*, and *finals* for clues to the meaning of each word. Take notes in the space below about how the words were used.

captain   If you are the captain of a team, you are the team's leader.
force   Force is the pushing or pulling effect that one thing has on another.
finals   In sports, the finals are the last games of a competition to show which team or player is best.

Collaborative Discussion

Work with a group to discuss the questions below. Give examples from *Bend It Like Bianca* to support your ideas. Take notes for your responses.

1 Why does Bianca offer to join the team?

2 What details show that Bianca has never played soccer before?

3 Review this part of the video: 1:45–2:42. What does Bianca learn to focus on when she kicks the ball?

Listening Tip

Turn toward the speaker as you listen. You will understand comments better if you can see the expression on the speaker's face and any gestures the person makes.

Speaking Tip

Say your words clearly and speak loudly enough to be heard. Look toward each listener to help you know if he or she understands what you say.

Write a Response

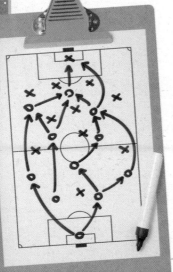

PROMPT ....

Respond to the Video In *Bend It Like Bianca*, you saw how the players on a soccer team must make sure everyone understands the game. How would you describe Kelly? How would you describe Bianca? How does Kelly help Bianca during their game? What happens after that? Cite evidence from the video to support your response.

EVIDENCE ....

List details from *Bend It Like Bianca* that describe Kelly and Bianca. Note how they work together and what happens as a result.

Now write your response in a paragraph.

Make sure your response

☐ uses evidence from the video to answer the questions.

☐ describes Kelly and Bianca.

☐ tells how the girls work together and what happens as a result.

☐ is written in complete sentences.

Notice &
Note
Contrasts and
Contradictions

Prepare to Read

GENRE STUDY **Realistic fiction** tells a story about characters and events that are like those in real life.

- Authors of realistic fiction tell the story through a plot that includes a conflict and its resolution.
- The events in realistic fiction build on each other.
- Realistic fiction includes characters who act, think, and speak like real people.
- Some realistic fiction includes a theme or lesson learned by the main character.

SET A PURPOSE **Think about** the title and genre of this text. This text is about a track meet. What do you know about track? What would you like to learn? Write your responses below.

CRITICAL VOCABULARY

meets

upset

concentrated

disappointed

personal

**Build Background:
Track Running**

BOUNCING BACK

1   My name is Amy Reid, and I was one of the top two track stars in the district. My biggest competition was Madison Palmer. During the last race of the season, I hurt my knee in a race against Madison, and I've been out for all of this track season.

2   Finally, my doctor gave me permission to start running again, just in time for our last two track meets. I was very nervous about whether or not my knee was actually healed. It didn't help when I saw Madison training one day and I heard her coach say she had run the lap in a minute and five seconds. That is faster than I could run the 400-meter dash when I was at my best.

3   I trained and practiced all weekend, but after trying my best at the first meet, I still came in third place. I had run my slowest race ever and wondered how I'd be ready for the race against Madison just three days later.

4   I went home and rushed right to my room. Almost immediately, my dad knocked on the door and asked me to come to the kitchen. Dad looked at me. We were both quiet for a long time. Finally, before I could change my mind, I told him everything.

5   I told him about my first thoughts of nervousness, about worrying about my knee, about seeing Madison in the park, about my false starts, and finally, about my really huge fear that I wouldn't be ready for Friday's meet. It was the final meet of the year. It was a really big deal.

meets   When swimmers or runners take part in races, the events are called meets.

6   "Madison has had two months of practice more than me," I finished. "She's been running faster than I've ever run. Today I tried as hard as I could and ran slower than ever."

7   Dad looked at me for a few seconds. He seemed to be thinking hard.

8   "Have you talked to Coach Joseph about any of this?" he asked finally.

9   "Dad, I haven't talked to anyone about any of this," I said.

10   "Oh, honey. I don't know what to tell you," Dad said with a sigh. "All you can do is your best. And you still have Friday's meet, right? I'm sure your slow run tonight was just you being nervous. Plus, you're still getting back into shape."

11   "Yeah," I said.

12   My dad didn't seem to understand how upset I was. I needed to talk to Natalie. My sister was always really good at solving problems.

13   "Dad?" I asked. "I need to talk to Natalie," I said. "No offense or anything," I added quickly.

14   "I understand, Amy. I'll go get her for you," Dad said as he stood up. He even looked a little relieved.

15   Soon, my sister walked into the kitchen.

16   "Okay, Amy," Natalie said, sitting down next to me. "Dad told me everything, and I have an idea."

17   She took a deep breath. Then she went on, "Why don't you go to the track in the park and talk to Madison? Maybe you can practice with her or something."

18   That wasn't exactly what I had in mind. "Are you kidding?" I asked.

19   "No, I'm not. She's just a girl who likes to run, like you are," said Natalie.

20   I sat for a few seconds to let the idea sink in. "Will you come with me?" I asked finally.

21   "Yeah," she said. Then she smiled. "I'm not running, though."

22   I laughed. "Deal," I said. "We'll go tomorrow after dinner."

---

upset   If you are upset, you are sad or unhappy about something.

MY BIGGEST COMPETITION

23   The next day, Natalie picked me up after practice. "Are you ready for tonight?" she asked.

24   "No," I said.

25   "Amy!" exclaimed Natalie. "We talked about this yesterday. Did you change your mind?"

26   "No," I said again. "Madison just makes me really nervous. She always wins."

27   "I bet she's just as impressed by you," said Natalie.

28   But I didn't think so.

29   After dinner, I put on my running clothes. Ten minutes later, Natalie and I were heading for the track.

30   As soon as we reached the track, I saw Madison. She was sprinting through the last hundred meters of a lap.

31   I started to turn around, but Natalie held onto my elbow and guided me toward the track.

32   Madison stopped running as we walked up. She squinted at us through the fence. "Amy Reid? Is that you?" she asked.

33   "Yeah," I said, surprised. "How do you know my name?"

34   Madison laughed. "Because you're my biggest competition!" she said. "What are you doing here?"

35   "Well, I live near here," I told her. "This is my sister, Natalie." Natalie and Madison smiled at each other.

36   I took a deep breath and went on, "So anyway, I was running near the track last week and saw you practicing." I looked at my sister for help.

37   "Amy had a rough meet last night. I suggested she come to ask you for some advice," Natalie said. "I mean, I know you're on different teams and everything, but . . ." She stopped. Madison had started to blush.

38   "Are you kidding?" asked Madison. "I should ask Amy for advice!"

39   I was shocked. "About what?" I asked.

40   "Your form!" Madison said. "Your form is always so perfect."

41   Then Natalie said, "If you two are going to practice, you should really get started."

42   Madison and I went to the starting line. We decided to run the first lap in our own styles, so that we could see the differences side-by-side.

43   We were really close for the first half, but I was in the lead.

44   I noticed that Madison's elbows seemed to fly out from her body a little. It was almost as if she was having trouble keeping her arms in close like you're supposed to.

45   We went around the second turn. That's when Madison sped up.

46   I tried to keep up with her, but I was out of energy. Plus, my knee was bugging me again.

47   Madison beat me by about two meters. That's a lot in such a short race.

48   After we caught our breath, I asked, "What's your secret?"

49   "I used to try to sprint the whole thing, but I was always so wiped out by the end. My coach suggested I try it a different way," Madison explained. "If you run a little slower than normal for the first half of the race, you can speed up for the second half and pass everyone." She shrugged. "It works really well."

50   I thought for a minute. "Okay," I said. "Let's run it again. This time I'll try it your way."

51 We ran another lap. That time, I actually beat her!

52 After we cooled down a little, I gave Madison some tips on keeping her elbows in close to her body. "See, I just pretend I'm on one of those ski machines, you know?" I told her. "Like on TV? It takes some getting used to, but keeping your elbows in really makes a difference."

53 Finally, I noticed that the sun was below the trees, so we decided to call it a night.

54 "See you Friday!" called Madison as Natalie and I headed back down the trail toward home.

55 "See you then!" I yelled back.

56 I felt happier than I had in days.

PERSONAL BEST

57   Friday morning was chilly and sunny. But by the time we changed and boarded the bus to drive to the meet, the sky had clouded over, the wind had picked up, and the rain was coming down in sheets.

58   The drive to Emeryville didn't take long, but it felt like forever.

59   The rain had let up a little by the time we got there, but the wind was still blowing. To make matters worse, it seemed like the rain and cold were making my knee stiff.

60   Soon, we arrived at the school. Little butterflies started to form in my stomach. I was so nervous.

61   This meet was a really important meet. Anyone who finished first or second in their event would compete in the State Finals.

62   I took my position in the lane. Madison was right next to me, in lane two. We smiled at each other.

63   "On your marks!"

64   I crouched down and faced forward.

65   "Get set!"

66   I pushed my toe as close as I could to the starting line without actually touching it.

67   *BANG!* The starting gun went off.

68   I **concentrated** all of my thoughts and effort on keeping up with Madison.

69   When we hit the second curve, Madison put on a burst of speed. I was surprised to find myself right next to her.

70   I was using Madison's method for running. So far, it was making a big difference. We were neck and neck. My knee hurt a little, but I ignored it. Then Madison pulled ahead. I pulled ahead of her for a few meters, but I couldn't keep my lead.

> **concentrated**   If you have concentrated on something, you have focused all your thoughts on it.

71 Suddenly, it was over. Madison had won.

72 For a second, I felt really disappointed. Yet again, Madison Palmer had beaten me.

73 But then Katie, my training partner, came running over. "Amy!" she called, sounding excited. "You ran a 1:05!"

74 "Are you serious?" I asked. I felt shocked. That was my fastest time ever. "Did I really?" I couldn't believe it. How had I run a 1:05 with a healing knee?

75 "Yeah, you really did," a girl's voice said.

76 I turned around. It was Madison. "Congratulations," I told her. "You were great."

> **disappointed**   If you are disappointed, you are sad that something didn't happen the way you wanted it to.

77 Madison smiled. "You were too! Personal best, right? Your best time ever?" she asked. "That's got to feel great!"

78 I smiled back. "Yes, it was," I admitted. "It feels pretty good."

79 Madison laughed. "Wait till the next meet," she said.

80 "You wait till the next meet," I joked. "Then my knee will be totally healed, and I'll be some serious competition!"

81 Everyone cheered as the official read our times into a microphone. I could see my dad and Natalie in the stands, jumping up and down.

82 "You already are serious competition," Madison said, smiling. "I can't wait till the next meet."

personal If something is personal, it is connected to and only about one person.

Collaborative Discussion

Look back at what you wrote on page 388. Tell a partner what you learned. Work with a group to discuss the questions below. Use details in *Running Rivals* to explain your answers. Take notes for your responses. After listening to others, restate the important ideas you heard before responding.

1 Reread pages 394–395. Why is Amy uneasy about talking to Madison?

> It is uneasy because Amy is realy nervouse because madison always wins

2 Review pages 396–398. What makes the meeting helpful for both runners?

> What makes it helpful for both runners is that they giving each other advice.

3 Which lesson from Madison helps Amy run her fastest time ever?

> She tells amy different tixpes of tips with keeping your arms close to your body.

Listening Tip

Listen for the main point each speaker makes. Think about how each idea can support or change what you think.

Speaking Tip

When sharing your thoughts, help listeners notice your key ideas. Be sure to use a complete sentence to state your most important idea.

Write a Response

PROMPT ··

Respond to the Text In *Running Rivals*, you read about two track stars who are also competitors. Why is Amy worried about her performance and about racing Madison? What happens during practice? In the end, how does the rivalry between Amy and Madison help both girls? Cite evidence from the text to support your response.

EVIDENCE ··

List details and ideas from *Running Rivals* that tell about the rivalry between Amy and Madison. Note what the girls learn from their rivalry.

WRITE

Now write your response in a paragraph.

Make sure your response

- ☐ uses evidence from the text to answer the questions.
- ☐ explains the rivalry between Amy and Madison.
- ☐ tells what the girls learn from their rivalry.
- ☐ is written in complete sentences.

Notice & Note
3 Big Questions

Prepare to Read

GENRE STUDY **Narrative nonfiction** gives factual information by telling a story.

- Narrative nonfiction presents events in chronological order, or in the order in which they happen.
- Narrative nonfiction includes real people.
- Narrative nonfiction may tell about historical events.

SET A PURPOSE **Think about** the title and genre of this text. The title includes the word *baseball*. What do you know about baseball? What would you like to learn? Write your responses below.

CRITICAL VOCABULARY

| littered |
| rivalry |
| disbanded |
| donated |
| generations |
| soared |

Meet the Author and Illustrator:
Audrey Vernick and Steven Salerno

THE TRUE STORY OF AN AMAZING ALL-BROTHER BASEBALL TEAM

BROTHERS AT BAT

written by Audrey Vernick
illustrated by Steven Salerno

I think this story is about a baseball team becal the guy in the cove in is holding a bat. And they bot like there winning

1   WHEN WINTER'S CHILL melts into spring, back doors swing open and slap shut as kids just home from school run outside—mitts, bats, and balls in hand.

2   In one New Jersey town near the ocean, back in the 1920s and '30s, you could hear the same door slam over and over. Three brothers raced out.

3   Out went three more.

4   And more:

5   And still more.

6   It sounds like a fairy tale: twelve baseball-playing brothers. But Anthony, Joe, Paul, Alfred, Charlie, Jimmy, Bobby, Billy, Freddie, Eddie, Bubbie, and Louie Acerra were real.

7   They had four sisters, too: Catherine, Florence, Rosina, and Frances. And a white dog . . . named Pitch! The sisters didn't play ball. Back then, most people thought sports were just for boys.

8 The Acerras had so many kids that they slept two to a bed and sat three across in their outdoor bathroom. They ate dinner wherever they could find a seat. Even on a baseball field, there were more boys than positions.

9 But that didn't stop them from playing.

10 Baseball set the rhythm of their lives.

11   "Every spring," Freddie said, "you would take your glove out, go in the yard, and play." Neighbors couldn't recall a time when there weren't Acerra boys outside tossing the ball, hitting it hard, racing around—with the young ones watching, wishing they were old enough to play.

12   Their high school baseball team had an Acerra on it twenty-two years in a row!

13   In 1938, the brothers ranged in age from seven to thirty-two. The oldest nine formed their own semi-pro team and competed against other New Jersey teams. Their father coached them and never missed a game.

14   Their uniforms all said the same thing:

Acerras.

1938

Anthony AGE 32

Joe AGE 27

Paul AGE 24

Alfred AGE 22

Charlie AGE 20

Jimmy AGE 18

Bobby AGE 16

Billy AGE 15

Freddie AGE 13

Eddie AGE 12

Bubbie AGE 10

Louie AGE 7

15   The infields they played on were dirt; outfields were littered with rocks and sand. The brothers loved to talk about the day they played at "the old dog track," an oceanfront stadium that had once been an auto raceway. It was there that Anthony, the oldest, hit a couple of home runs right into the Atlantic Ocean.

16   They called Anthony "Poser" because of the way he'd stand at the plate—as if his baseball-card photo were being taken.

17   Charlie, the fifth oldest, was the slowest brother. He was a good player, but a terrible runner. The brothers often joked about the time he hit a ball nearly out of the park, but only made it to second.

18   Jimmy, the sixth brother, had a knuckleball people *still* talk about. "You couldn't hit it," Eddie said. "You couldn't catch it, either." That ball danced in the air. Jimmy was a great hitter, too, probably the best player on the team.

> **littered**   If an area is littered with items, those items are scattered all around.

19   But there was no jealousy, no rivalry, no fighting. As the younger brothers grew up, the older ones shared playing time. If someone dropped a fly ball or struck out, no one screamed or threw down his glove or stomped off the field. "We stuck together," Freddie said.

20   The team played around New Jersey, in New York, Connecticut, wherever they could find a good game. Paul sent out letters, looking for new teams to play. The all-brother team always drew big crowds.

rivalry   A rivalry is a competition between teams or people who want to win the same thing.

21   In 1939, at the New York World's Fair, the Acerras were honored as the biggest family in New Jersey. They were taken to the Newark airport, where they boarded a plane and were flown over the fairgrounds. They couldn't believe it—no one they knew had been on a plane before! Most of the people at the World's Fair, looking up at that small plane in the sky, had no idea there was a whole team of brothers aboard.

22   But it wasn't all fun and games and sunny skies. Their darkest day occurred on the field, too.

i think he will get hurt and go to the doctor.

23   Freddie was on third base in a scoreless game. Alfred was at
the plate. He touched his shoulder—the signal that he was
going to bunt.

24   Then things went wrong.

25   The pitch came in high, and somehow the ball bounced
off the bat and hit Alfred hard, right in the face.

26   They rushed him to the doctor, but he lost an eye.

27   For the next few months, Eddie took Alfred's place as
catcher. Everyone thought Alfred's baseball days were over.

28   But when you have eleven brothers willing to throw you
balls in the yard—gently at first, then a bit harder—you get
your skills back. You get your courage back, too. Alfred was
soon wearing the Acerras uniform again.

29   "He was a pretty good catcher for a guy
with one eye," Freddie said.

30   In the 1940s, something pulled the brothers' attention away from baseball. American soldiers were fighting in the Second World War across the Atlantic—that same huge ocean Poser had hit baseballs into.

31   Battles were raging and soldiers were dying, but the brothers knew it was important to fight for their country.

32   The team disbanded as six Acerra brothers joined the service. Poser was the first to go. He, Charlie, Eddie, and Bobby all served in the Army. After Billy joined the Marines, Freddie did, too.

disbanded   If a group disbanded, its members no longer work together.

33   Those six brothers traveled far from home. After a lifetime of talking and playing together every day, they now went months—years!—without seeing one another. They longed for the salty-stew smell of the Atlantic Ocean.

34   They dreamed of their childhood home, of the back door *slap slap slapping* as they ran outside to play. And of long afternoons, throwing a ball in high, soaring arcs from glove to glove to glove in a field full of brothers.

35   Back in New Jersey, their parents and siblings waited for news. It took a long time for letters to reach them from overseas. There was a lot of time to worry.

36   When the war finally ended, everyone was so happy. Eddie, out in California with the Army, was so excited that he went up to women he didn't even know and kissed them!

37   Many American soldiers died in World War II, but the Acerras were very lucky. One by one, all six brothers returned from their time in the service. Mama Acerra cried each time a boy walked in the door.

38   By the summer of 1946, the family was ready to get back to baseball. They were all older, of course, and Poser's heart had grown weak, so now he coached the team.

39   They joined the Long Branch City Twilight Baseball League and over the next six years won the league championship four times.

40   Every Sunday, crowds filled the stands to watch the all-brother team play.

1947

1948

1949

1950

41   As time passed, the Acerras got married and
moved into their own homes. They worked hard at
their jobs—at the water company, at the post office,
selling insurance. They started having children of
their own.

42   In 1952, they played their last game as a team.
But they had already made history.

43   The Acerra brothers were the longest-playing
all-brother baseball team ever.

44   In 1997, the Baseball Hall of Fame held a special ceremony to honor them. Only seven were still alive. Paul, Alfred, Bobby, Billy, Freddie, Eddie, and Bubbie all made the trip, along with more than a hundred relatives, including their sister Frances.

45   Jimmy's son donated his father's uniform and glove, which were put on display, right there in the same museum that honored Babe Ruth and Ty Cobb and Willie Mays. "They treated us like we were kings," Freddie said.

> **donated**   Something that is donated is freely given as a gift to a charity, organization, or other group.

46   After such a thrilling day, you could picture them driving off into the sunset, happily ever after.

47   But their bus broke down.

48   They could have sat on the curb, grumbling in the summer heat. But someone found a bat and ball, and as three generations of Acerras waited for a new bus, they played ball.

49   That ball soared from grandfather to granddaughter, from father to son.

50   From brother to brother.

> **generations**   A generation is all the people in a family, social group, or country that are about the same age.
>
> **soared**   If something soared, it flew quickly through the air.

Collaborative Discussion

Look back at what you wrote on page 406. Tell a partner what you learned. Work with a group to discuss the questions below. Refer to details in *Brothers at Bat* for your answers. Take notes for your responses. Share your ideas as you discuss.

1 Review pages 411–412. What details show that baseball was important to the Acerra family?

> It was important because they now to go ogant other teams

2 Reread page 417. How do the Acerra brothers help Alfred return to baseball after his injury?

> They helped him by giving him courage and love.

3 How did the Acerra brothers' lives change as time went on? In what ways did the family stay the same?

> The _____ st__t _____

Listening Tip

Listen politely and look at the person who is speaking. Wait until the speaker is finished before sharing your ideas.

Speaking Tip

Look at the other members of your group when you speak. Speak clearly and loudly enough so that everyone can hear you.

Write a Response

Respond to the Text In *Brothers at Bat*, you read the true story of twelve brothers who played baseball together throughout their lives. What other events took place in the Acerras' lives? How did this family demonstrate teamwork? Cite evidence from the text to support your response.

EVIDENCE

List the events and details from *Brothers at Bat* that tell about important events in the Acerras' lives. Note how the family demonstrated teamwork.

WRITE

Now write your response in a paragraph.

✓	**Make sure your response**
☐	uses evidence from the text to answer the questions.
☐	tells about events in the lives of the Acerra brothers.
☐	explains how the family demonstrated teamwork.
☐	is written in complete sentences.

? **Essential Question**

What can sports teach us about working together?

Write an Expository Essay

PROMPT Think about how the characters and people in this module worked together to accomplish a goal. What challenges did they face? What lesson did they learn about teamwork? Write an expository essay that explains how the authors use sports to teach readers about teamwork. Use evidence from the module selections in your ideas.

✓ **Make sure your expository essay**

☐ introduces the topic.

☐ explains how authors use sports to teach us about working together.

☐ describes the challenges the characters face and the lessons they learn about teamwork.

☐ uses text evidence from the selections.

☐ provides a conclusion.

.... Map your ideas.

How do the characters work together to accomplish a goal? What
challenges do they face? What lessons do they learn about teamwork? Use
the map below to plan your writing.

Examples of Teamwork	Challenges	Lessons

DRAFT .... Write your expository essay.

Use the information you wrote on page 429 to draft your expository essay.
Write a beginning paragraph that introduces your topic.

Write one or more paragraphs that explain how authors use sports to
teach readers about teamwork. Use text evidence to support your ideas.
Connect your ideas with transition words and phrases.

Write a conclusion that summarizes your ideas.

The revising and editing steps give you a chance to look carefully at your writing and make changes. Work with a partner to determine whether you have explained your ideas. Use the questions below to help you.

PURPOSE/FOCUS	ORGANIZATION	EVIDENCE/SUPPORT	ELABORATION	CONVENTIONS
☐ Do I answer the questions? ☐ Do I explain how authors use sports to teach readers about teamwork?	☐ Do I have a clear introduction to the topic? ☐ Does my conclusion summarize my topic?	☐ Have I used text evidence to support my ideas?	☐ Have I explained my ideas clearly? ☐ Have I used transitions to connect my ideas?	☐ Have I spelled all words correctly? ☐ Have I used correct end marks? ☐ Have I used capitalization correctly?

PUBLISH ···················· Create a finished copy.

Make a final copy of your expository essay. Use your cursive writing skills.

431

Glossary

This glossary contains meanings and pronunciations for some of the words in this book. The Full Pronunciation Key shows how to pronounce each consonant and vowel in a special spelling. At the bottom of the glossary pages is a shortened form of the full key.

Full Pronunciation Key

CONSONANT SOUNDS

b	**b**i**b**, ca**bb**age	r	**r**oar, **rh**yme
ch	**ch**ur**ch**, sti**tch**	s	mi**ss**, **s**au**c**e,
d	**d**ee**d**, mail**ed**,		**sc**ene, **s**ee
	pu**dd**le	sh	di**sh**, **sh**ip, **s**ugar,
f	**f**ast, **f**i**f**e, o**ff**,		ti**ss**ue
	phrase, rou**gh**	t	**t**ight, stopp**ed**
g	**g**a**g**, **g**et, fin**g**er	th	ba**th**, **th**in
h	**h**at, **wh**o	th	ba**th**e, **th**is
hw	**wh**ich, **wh**ere	v	ca**v**e, **v**al**v**e, **v**ine
j	**j**u**dg**e, **g**em	w	**w**ith, **w**olf
k	**c**at, **k**i**ck**, s**ch**ool	y	**y**es, **y**olk, on**i**on
kw	**ch**oir, **qu**ick	z	ro**s**e, si**z**e,
l	**l**id, need**le**, ta**ll**		**x**ylophone,
m	a**m**, **m**an, du**mb**		**z**ebra
n	**n**o, sudd**en**	zh	gara**g**e,
ng	thi**ng**, i**nk**		plea**s**ure, vi**s**ion
p	**p**op, ha**pp**y		

VOWEL SOUNDS

ă	p**a**t, l**au**gh	ô	**a**ll, **c**augh**t**, **for**,
ā	**a**pe, **ai**d, p**ay**		p**aw**
â	**air**, **c**a**re**, w**ear**	oi	b**oy**, n**oi**se, **oil**
ä	f**a**ther, k**oa**la,	ou	c**ow**, **ou**t
	y**ar**d	ŏŏ	f**u**ll, b**oo**k, w**o**lf
ĕ	p**e**t, pl**ea**sure,	ōō	b**oo**t, r**u**de, fr**ui**t,
	any		fl**ew**
ē	b**e**, b**ee**, **ea**sy,	ŭ	c**u**t, fl**oo**d,
	p**ia**no		r**ou**gh, s**o**me
ĭ	**i**f, p**i**t, b**u**sy	û	c**ir**cle, f**ur**, h**ear**d,
ī	r**i**de, b**y**, p**ie**,		t**er**m, t**ur**n, **ur**ge,
	h**igh**		w**or**d
î	d**ear**, d**eer**,	yŏŏ	c**u**re
	f**ie**rce, m**ere**	yōō	ab**u**se, **u**se
ŏ	h**o**rrible, p**o**t	ə	**a**go, sil**e**nt,
ō	g**o**, r**ow**, t**oe**,		penc**i**l, lem**o**n,
	th**ough**		circ**u**s

STRESS MARKS

Primary Stress ´: biology [bī•**ŏl**´•ə•jē]

Secondary Stress ´: biological [bī´•ə•**lŏj**´•ĭ•kəl]

A

ability (ə•**bĭl′**•ĭ•tē) *n.* If you have the ability to do something, you can do it because you know how. I have the ability to play many different types of characters.

actor (**ăk′**•tər) *n.* An actor is a person who acts in plays, movies, or other performances. I dream of being an actor who can perform in plays, movies, and musicals.

annual (**ăn′**•yo͞o•əl) *adj.* An annual event happens once each year. The whole family looks forward to Aunt Betty's annual harvest feast.

apprehensive (ăp′•rĭ•**hĕn′**•sĭv) *adj.* If you are apprehensive, you are worried something bad might happen. I told my mom that I was apprehensive about my first day of school.

assigned (ə•**sīnd′**) *v.* If someone assigned a task to you, he or she gave you some work to do. The teacher assigned a lesson for us to complete together.

audition (ô•**dĭsh′**•ən) *n.* When actors or musicians go to an audition, they give a performance to show what they can do. I have an audition for the lead role in our school play.

B

backdrop (**băk′**•drŏp) *n.* On a stage, a backdrop is a painted curtain or wall that shows the setting of the scene. The backdrop was painted to show scenery with clouds, mountains, and trees.

Baroque (bə•**rōk′**) *adj.* The Baroque period was many years ago. The buildings of that time were very fancy and decorated. The palace was from the Baroque period.

bilingual (bī•**lĭng′**•gwəl) *adj.* People who are bilingual can speak two languages. The new student is bilingual, speaking English with us at school and speaking Korean with her family at home.

Word Origins

bilingual The word *bilingual* is from the mid-19th century Latin word *bilinguis*, with *bi–* meaning "having two" and *lingua* meaning "tongue." *Bi–* is a prefix that occurs in other English words such as *bicycle* and *bifold*.

---

block (blŏk) *n.* A block is a section of a community with streets on all of its sides. My best friend lives on the same neighborhood block as I do.

---

o͞o b**oo**t / ou **ou**t / ŭ c**u**t / û f**u**r / hw **wh**ich / th **th**in / *th* **th**is / zh vi**s**ion / ə **a**go, sil**e**nt, penc**i**l, lem**o**n, circ**u**s

breezy (**brē'**•zē) *adj.* When it is breezy outside, you can feel the wind softly blowing. It is a breezy day, which is perfect for flying a kite.

broad (brôd) *adj.* Something that is broad is wide. My dad and I flew our kite in the broad field.

burden (**bûr'**•dn) *n.* A burden is something that is heavy to carry. My backpack, books, and school supplies were a burden to carry home on the last day of school.

C

captain (**kăp'**•tən) *n.* If you are the captain of a team, you are the team's leader. The captain of the soccer team carried the trophy after the game.

chronicle (**krŏn'**•ĭ•kəl) *n.* A chronicle is a story or account of a series of events. We read a chronicle about how Sacagawea helped Lewis and Clark travel west.

civic (**sĭv'**•ĭk) *adj.* The word *civic* describes the duties, rights, and responsibilities of citizens in a community, city, or nation. Elected officials do their civic duty by serving our nation.

clash (klăsh) *v.* Colors or patterns that clash look strange or ugly together. My mom thinks the things in Grandma's house clash, but I like seeing all the colorful patterns and objects.

coiled (koild') *v.* If you coiled something, you shaped it into loops or rings. Clara coiled the hose after she was finished watering the plants.

collaboration (kə•lăb'•ə•**rā'**•shən) *n.* Collaboration is working together in a group to accomplish a task. Our football team uses collaboration to perform plays given to us by our coach.

competition (kŏm'•pĭ•**tĭsh'**•ən) *n.* If you are in a competition, you are in a contest against another person or team. Tug of war is a fun competition between the third grade classrooms.

concentrated (**kŏn'**•sən•trā'•tĭd) *v.* If you have concentrated on something, you have focused all your thoughts on it. I concentrated very hard on my math homework to prepare for the big test.

conductor (kən•**dŭk'**•tər) *n.* A conductor directs a group of people who sing or play musical instruments. Our music conductor makes sure that we are singing the right words at the right time.

consult (kən•**sŭlt'**) *v.* If you consult something, you look at it to find information. We needed to consult the map to find the island.

ă r**at** / ā **pay** / â c**are** / ä f**a**ther / ĕ p**e**t / ē be / ĭ p**i**t / ī p**ie** / î f**ie**rce / ŏ p**o**t / ō g**o** / ô p**aw**, f**o**r / oi **oi**l / ŏŏ b**oo**k /

D

convention (kən•**věn'**•shən) *n.* A convention is a meeting of people who share the same purpose or ideas. Sophia and her family went to the convention to view the exhibits and to listen to the speakers.

convey (kən•**vā'**) *v.* When you convey information or feelings, you communicate or make an idea understandable to someone. The teacher will convey what he expects of his students.

costumes (**kŏs'**•tōomz) *n.* Costumes are special clothes that people may wear to pretend that they are from another time or place. We wore animal costumes for our school play.

creative (krē•**ā'**•tĭv) *adj.* Someone who is creative can imagine ideas and invent new things. Artists are very creative people.

deceive (dĭ•**sēv'**) *v.* If you deceive others, you tell a lie or try to make them believe something that is not true. My friend tried to deceive his father, but his father did not believe the lie.

Word Origins

deceive The word *deceive* is from the Latin word *decipere*, which means "to catch or cheat."

declaring (dĭ•**klâr'**•ĭng) *v.* When you are declaring something, you feel strongly about it and are making it clearly known. The politician is declaring the changes he will make if he wins the election.

deflected (də•**flĕk'**•tĭd) *v.* If you deflected something that was moving, you made it go in a different direction. The goalie deflected the ball away from the net.

delegates (**dĕl'**•ĭ•gĭts) *n.* People who have been chosen to make decisions for a larger group are called delegates. Ms. Campton is one of the delegates that represent the teachers from our school.

democracy (dĭ•**mŏk'**•rə•sē) *n.* A democracy is a kind of government in which the people choose leaders by voting. In the United States, we vote for our president because we are a democracy.

demolition (dĕm'•ə•**lĭsh'**•ən) *n.* If you work in demolition, your job is to tear down or destroy buildings. The demolition of the old building is happening now.

desires (dĭ•**zīrz'**) *n.* Your desires are your wishes for certain things to happen. One of Derek's desires in life is to become a police officer.

ōō b**oo**t / ou **ou**t / ŭ c**u**t / û f**u**r / hw **wh**ich / th **th**in / th **th**is / zh vi**s**ion / ə **a**go, sil**e**nt, penc**i**l, lem**o**n, circ**u**s

determination
(dĭ•tûr′•mə•**nā′**•shən) *n.* When you keep trying until you succeed, you show determination. The athlete showed determination to finish the race.

disappointed (dĭs′•ə•**poin′**•tĭd) *adj.* If you are disappointed, you are sad that something didn't happen the way that you wanted it to. I was disappointed that I could not play outside today.

disbanded (dĭs•**băn′**•dĭd) *v.* If a group disbanded, its members no longer work together. Fans were very upset when their favorite musical group disbanded.

distract (dĭ•**străkt′**) *v.* If you distract someone, you focus attention away from something. Alyssa made faces to distract her little brother during his check-up.

domestic (də•**mĕs′**•tĭk) *adj.* When something is domestic, it is part of or about the country in which you live. The Fourth of July is a domestic holiday that celebrates the United States of America.

donated (dō′•nā•təd) *v.* Something that is donated is freely given as a gift to a charity, organization, or other group. We donated the clothes that we packed into the box.

drastic (**drăs′**•tĭk) *adj.* If you make a drastic change, you do something very different from what you have always done. Painting helped to make a drastic change to the color of my bedroom.

drowsy (**drou′**•zē) *adj.* A drowsy person is sleepy and not able to think clearly. My little brother was very drowsy while he was trying to read his book.

E

emergency (ĭ•**mûr′**•jən•sē) *n.* An emergency is an unexpected situation that requires help or quick action to make it better. The fire truck races to the scene of the emergency.

eminent (**ĕm′**•ə•nənt) *adj.* An eminent person is famous and important. Abraham Lincoln was an eminent person who believed that people should be treated fairly.

endowed (ĕn•**doud′**) *v.* If you have been endowed with a feature or quality, it is yours and belongs to you. The baby was endowed at birth with a cheerful nature.

Word Origins

endowed The word *endowed* is from the old French word *endouer*, *en–* "in towards" and *douer* "give as a gift."

---

entry (**ĕn′**•trē) *n.* If you write an entry, you write a short note in a diary or a book. Olivia wrote an entry in her diary each day after school.

ă r**a**t / ā p**ay** / â c**a**re / ä f**a**ther / ĕ p**e**t / ē b**e** / ĭ p**i**t / ī p**ie** / î f**ie**rce / ŏ p**o**t / ō g**o** / ô p**aw, fo**r / oi **oi**l / o͝o b**oo**k /

express (ĭk•**sprĕs′**) *v.* When you express yourself, you show what you feel and think. Their smiles express that they are happy to be at the party.

F

feature (**fē′**•chər) *n.* A feature is an important or interesting part of a person or thing. I named my puppy Spot after his most noticeable feature.

ferry (**fĕr′**•ē) *n.* A ferry is a boat that takes people or vehicles across a river or waterway. The best part of our family vacation was the ride on the ferry.

finals (**fī′**•nəlz) *n.* In sports, the finals are the last games of a competition to show which team or player is best. The two best teams played in the finals and we won!

force (fôrs) *n.* Force is the pushing or pulling effect that one thing has on another. Aiden pushed the swing with enough force to make Zoey feel like she was flying.

G

generations (jĕn′•ə•**rā′**•shənz) *n.* A generation is all the people in a family, social group, or country that are about the same age. There are three generations in my family.

genuine (**jĕn′**•yoo•ĭn) *adj.* If something is genuine, it is real and exactly what it seems to be. Seeing her father return filled the girl with genuine happiness.

greedily (**grēd′**•ə•lē) *adv.* When you do something greedily, you take more than you need. The boys greedily reached for the food.

gritty (**grĭt′**•ē) *adj.* When something feels gritty, it feels rough and sandy. My feet and legs were covered with gritty sand from the beach.

H

hesitation (hĕz′•ĭ•**tā′**•shən) *n.* A hesitation is a pause that shows you are unsure about doing something. Lucy continued reading after a slight hesitation.

hoisted (**hois′**•tĕd) *v.* If you hoisted a flag, you used ropes to pull it up a pole. The cadets hoisted the flag up the pole this morning.

hydrant (**hī′**•drənt) *n.* A hydrant is an outdoor pipe firefighters use to get water to put out fires. The red fire hydrant was easy to see in the snow.

— **Word Origins** —

hydrant The word *hydrant* is from the early 19th century root *hydro,* which means "relating to water."

ōō b**oo**t / ou **ou**t / ŭ c**u**t / û f**u**r / hw **wh**ich / th **th**in / *th* **th**is / zh vi**s**ion / ə **a**go, sil**e**nt, penc**i**l, lem**o**n, circ**u**s

I

illustrate (ĭl'•ə•strāt) *v.* If you illustrate a book, you draw pictures that go with the story. Our teacher told us to write and illustrate our stories.

independence (ĭn'•dĭ•**pĕn'**•dəns) *n.* If you are free to set your own rules and make your own choices, you have independence. Our teacher gave us the independence to choose our own reading partners this year.

individuality (ĭn'•də•vĭj'•ōō•**ăl'**•ĭ•tē) *n.* Your individuality is what makes you different from everyone else. Our teacher reminds us to respect each student's individuality.

inspired (ĭn•**spīrd'**) *v.* If an idea or action inspired you, it made you want to do something. After meeting him, I was inspired to become a firefighter.

intercepted (ĭn'•tər•**sĕp'**•tĭd) *v.* If you intercepted something, you stopped it from getting to where it was going. He intercepted a pass to take the football away from the other team.

L

littered (lĭt'•ərd) *adj.* If an area is littered with items, those items are scattered all around the area. The room was littered with toys.

loyal (loi'•əl) *adj.* When you are loyal to someone or something, you strongly support it. The loyal fans cheered when the team scored.

M

march (märch) *v.* When people march, they walk with even steps, often in a group. Royal guards march outside of the palace.

meets (mēts) *n.* When swimmers or runners take part in races, the events are called meets. During track meets, the athletes must hold a position before starting each race.

merciful (**mûr'**•sĭ•fəl) *adj.* Someone who is merciful is kind and forgiving. If I do something wrong, my father is merciful and always accepts my apology.

mismatched (**mĭs'**•măchd) *adj.* Things that are mismatched do not fit or belong together. Carla loves wearing mismatched socks to school each day.

Word Origins

mismatched The prefix *mis–* is from Old and Middle English *mes–*, and *mis–* means "bad" or "wrong." Thus the word *mismatched* means that things are wrongly or badly matched.

ă rat / ā pay / â care / ä father / ĕ pet / ē be / ĭ pit / ī pie / î fierce / ŏ pot / ō go / ô paw, for / oi oil / ōo book /

monument (**mŏn'**•yŏŏ•mənt) *n.* A monument is a large statue or building that honors an important person or event in history. We like to walk past the monument in the park.

moody (**mōō'**•dē) *adj.* If you are moody, your feelings change often and quickly. When people are feeling moody, they might feel happy one minute and sad the next.

mosaics (mō•**zā'**•ĭks) *n.* Mosaics are pictures or patterns made from smaller pieces of glass, stone, or other materials. We saw the brightly colored mosaics on the wall.

mushy (**mŭsh'**•ē) *adj.* Something that is mushy is soft and squishy. My mom poured the mushy peas in a bowl.

P

peasant (**pĕz'**•ənt) *n.* A peasant is someone who is very poor and may work as a farmer. The peasant worked in the fields planting corn.

performance (pər•**fôr'**•məns) *n.* If you sing, dance, or speak in front of a group, you give a performance. Sue Lynn practiced for weeks to get ready for her performance.

personal (**pûr'**•sə•nəl) *adj.* If something is personal, it is connected to and only about one person. My dad has a personal trainer at the gym.

Word Origins

personal The word *person* is from the Latin word *persōne*. Both *personal* and *personality* come from the same Latin root word relating to a person.

personality (pûr'•sə•**năl'**•ĭ•tē) *n.* Your personality is your nature or all the ways you think, feel, and act. My parents say that my brother and I each have our own personality.

pesky (**pĕs'**•kē) *adj.* Something that is pesky is annoying. Mom tried to swat the pesky bug in our house.

posterity (pŏ•**stĕr'**•ĭ•tē) *n.* If you think ahead about all the people who will be alive in the future, you are thinking about posterity. We have a family portrait that we keep for posterity.

precious (**prĕsh'**•əs) *adj.* If something is precious to you, it is important or valuable to you. Julia's doll was precious to her because she received it from her mother on the day she was born.

ōō b**oo**t / ou **ou**t / ŭ c**u**t / û f**u**r / hw **wh**ich / th **th**in / th **th**is / zh vi**s**ion / ə **a**go, sil**e**nt, penc**i**l, lem**o**n, circ**u**s

predictable (prĭ•**dĭkt'**•ə•bəl) *adj.* If something is predictable, it is just what you expect, with no surprises. Math sentences have a predictable pattern that is followed to find the solution.

presented (prĭ•**zĕn'**•tĭd) *v.* If you presented something, you showed it or gave it to someone. I presented my book report to the class.

projects (**prŏj'**•ĕktzs') *n.* Projects are tasks that take time and effort to complete. The students presented their projects at the science fair.

protested (**prō'**•tĕs'•tĭd) *v.* If you protested, you said why you did not agree with a statement or an idea. The workers protested when they disagreed with the company's new policies.

pulleys (**pŏŏl'**•ēz) *n.* Pulleys are wheels wrapped with rope that people can use to lift heavy objects. My uncle used pulleys to help him hoist up the engine of his car.

R

reassuring (rē'•ə•**shŏŏr'**•ĭng) *v.* If you are reassuring a friend, you are trying to keep him from worrying about something. Alexa kept reassuring her brother that he would find his lost baseball card.

recited (rĭ•**sī'**•tĭd) *v.* If you recited something, you said it aloud after you had learned it. Lucas had practiced the speech in his head, but he felt nervous as he recited it in front of the class.

rehearse (rĭ•**hûrs'**) *v.* If you rehearse a play, song, or dance, you practice it many times so that you are prepared. The drama teacher helped the students rehearse their lines before opening night.

Word Origins

rehearse The Latin prefix *re–* means "again." So the word *rehearse* means to "practice again." *Re–* is used in other words such as *recycle*, *refresh*, and *reuse*.

retains (rĭ•**tānz'**) *v.* If someone retains something, he or she has something and keeps it. Martia retains the award she won from the spelling bee contest.

rivalry (**rī'**•vəl•rē) *n.* A rivalry is a competition between teams or people who want to win the same thing. The players competed in the soccer rivalry between the two teams.

ă r**a**t / ā p**ay** / â c**a**re / ä f**a**ther / ĕ p**e**t / ē b**e** / ĭ p**i**t / ī p**ie** / î f**ie**rce / ŏ p**o**t / ō g**o** / ô p**aw**, f**or** / oi **oi**l / ŏŏ b**oo**k /

S

saga (**sä′•**gə) *n.* A saga is a long, detailed story about heroic events. Greg hoped to get to the next chapter in the saga before bedtime.

scrunches (**skrŭnch′•**ĕs) *v.* If something scrunches up, it is squeezed or crushed into a different shape. Sometimes my sister scrunches up her messy writing assignments.

sculptor (**skŭlp′•**tər) *n.* A sculptor is an artist who uses stone, wood, or metal to make a work of art. The sculptor worked very hard to create a beautiful stone statue for the new park.

snarled (snärld) *v.* If something is snarled, it is twisted and tangled. The colored thread was all snarled together.

soared (sôrd) *v.* If something soared, it flew quickly through the air. The eagle soared across the clear blue sky.

sovereignty (**sŏv′•**rĭn•tē) *n.* Sovereignty is the right and power a nation has to rule itself or another country or state. The Founding Fathers wanted America to have sovereignty, or independence, from British Rule.

speed (spēd) *v.* If you speed, you move too fast. The skater will speed past the others on the road.

sprawling (**sprôl′•**ĭng) *adj.* If you move in a sprawling way, you spread out your arms and legs. Gabby moves in a sprawling way on the leaves as she looks up at the sky.

stately (**stāt′**lē) *adj.* When something is stately, it is awesome or grand. The U.S. Capitol is a stately building.

steep (stēp) *adj.* If a hill or mountain is steep, it is difficult to climb because it goes almost straight up. They rode their bikes down the steep mountain.

suggest (səg•**jĕst′**) *v.* If you suggest something, you give ideas or plans for someone to think about. We were excited when our teacher let us suggest ideas for the class play.

superior (soo•**pîr′•**ē•ər) *adj.* Someone who is superior at something is more skilled than others. Marta won the first-place award, which is superior to the other contest awards.

symbiosis (sĭm′•bē•**ō′•**sĭs) *n.* Symbiosis happens when two individuals closely work together and both benefit from it. Crystal and I have a symbiosis on the volleyball court that helped us get to the championship finals.

T

tame (tām) *v.* If you tame a wild animal, you teach it to do what you want. The trainer's job is to tame the horses by teaching them to follow commands.

ōo b**oo**t / ou **ou**t / ŭ c**u**t / û f**u**r / hw **wh**ich / th **th**in / *th* **th**is / zh vi**s**ion / ə **a**go, sil**e**nt, penc**i**l, lem**o**n, circ**u**s

technical (tĕk'•nĭ•kəl) *adj.* The technical parts of a sport are the basic skills and understandings that are needed to play. In soccer practice, our coach helps us develop our technical skills.

torch (tôrch) *n.* A torch is a long stick with a flame at one end that may be used for light or to start a fire. The flaming torch was held high in the air.

U

unique (yōo•nēk') *adj.* Something or someone that is unique is one of a kind. Each snowflake has a unique shape.

unity (yōo'•nĭ•tē) *n.* Unity is when people join together for a common idea or cause. We joined our hands together in unity before the game.

unnoticed (ŭn•nō'•tĭsd) *adj.* If something is unnoticed, it is not seen by anyone. The dog went unnoticed as Carrie talked on the phone.

upset (ŭp•sĕt') *adj.* If you are upset, you are sad or unhappy about something. Ashley was very upset, but her mom tried to cheer her up.

usual (yōo'•zhōo•əl) *adj.* The usual way to do something is the way that it is done most often. Wan's usual routine is to brush his teeth each morning before school.

V

venturing (vĕn'•chər•ĭng) *v.* If you are venturing somewhere, you are going somewhere that is unfamiliar and may be unsafe. We were venturing down an unfamiliar trail.

video (vĭd'•ē•ō) *n.* The word *video* describes a recording of movements and actions that you can see on a television or computer screen. My family enjoys watching the video my dad made from our last vacation.

W

welfare (wĕl'•fâr) *n.* If someone looks out for your welfare, that person makes sure you are healthy and happy. In a hospital, doctors and nurses look out for the welfare of their patients.

whirled (wûrld) *v.* If something whirled, it spun and turned very quickly. The water whirled in a circle under the bridge.

winking (wĭngk'•ĭng) *v.* You are winking when you quickly blink one eye at someone because you share a joke or secret. Ethan was winking at his little sister as he snuck her a treat before dinnertime.

ă r**a**t / ā p**ay** / â c**a**re / ä f**a**ther / ĕ p**e**t / ē b**e** / ĭ p**i**t / ī p**ie** / î f**ie**rce / ŏ p**o**t / ō g**o** / ô p**aw**, f**or** / oi **oi**l / ŏŏ b**oo**k /

Index of Titles and Authors

Index of Titles and Authors

Acknowledgments

Brothers At Bat by Audrey Vernick, illustrated by Steven Salerno. Text copyright © 2012 by Audrey Vernick. Illustrations copyright © 2012 by Steven Salerno. Reprinted by permission of Houghton Mifflin Harcourt Publishing Company.

Dear Primo by Dunkin Tonatiuh. Copyright © 2010 by Dunkin Tonatiuh. Reprinted by permission of Express Permissions on behalf of Abrams Books for Young Readers, in imprint of Harry N. Abrams, Inc.

Dear Dragon by Josh Funk. Illustrated by Rodolfo Montalvo. Text copyright © 2016 by Josh Funk. Illustrations copyright © 2016 by Rodolfo Montalvo. Reprinted by permission of Viking Children's Books, an imprint of Penguin Young Readers Group, a division of Penguin Random House LLC. All rights reserved. Any third party use of this material, outside of this publication, is prohibited. Interested parties must apply directly to Penguin Random House LLC for permission.

The Flag Maker by Susan Campbell Bartoletti, illustrated by Claire A. Nivola. Text copyright © 2004 by Susan Campbell Bartoletti. Illustrations copyright © 2004 by Claire A. Nivola. Reprinted by permission of Houghton Mifflin Harcourt Publishing Company.

Excerpt from *I Can't Accept Not Trying: Michael Jordan on the Pursuit of Excellence* by Michael Jordan. Copyright © 1994 by Rare Air, Ltd. Text copyright © 1994 by Michael Jordan. Reprinted by permission of HarperCollins Publishers and Rare Air, Ltd.

"I, Like You" by Casey Hermansson, illustrated by Susan Farrington from *Cricket* Magazine, February 2012. Text copyright © 2012 by Carus Publishing Company. Art copyright © 2012 by Susan Farrington. Reprinted by permission of Cricket Media. All Cricket Media material is copyrighted by Carus Publishing d/b/a Cricket Media, and/or various authors and illustrators. Any commercial use or distribution of material without permission is strictly prohibited. Please visit http://www.cricketmedia.com/info/licensing2 for licensing and http://www.cricketmedia.com for subscriptions.

"I Go to the Land", "In the Land of Words", "Jokes", and "Riddles" from *In the Land of Words: New and Selected Poems* by Eloise Greenfield, illustrated by Jan Spivey Gilchrist. Text copyright © 2004 by Eloise Greenfield. Illustrations copyright © 2004 by Jan Spivey Gilchrist. Reprinted by permission of HarperCollins Publishers.

Judy Moody, Mood Martian by Megan McDonald, illustrated by Peter H. Reynolds. Text copyright © 2014 by Megan McDonald. Illustrations copyright © 2014 by Peter H. Reynolds. Reproduced by permission of the publisher, Candlewick Press and Brilliance Audio.

Marisol McDonald Doesn't Match by Monica Brown, illustrated by Sara Palacios. Text copyright © 2011 by Monica Brown. Illustrations copyright © 2011 by Sara Palacios. Reprinted by permission of Children's Book Press, an imprint of Lee & Low Books Inc.

Excerpt from *Running Rivals* by Jake Maddox/Val Priebe, illustrated by Tuesday Morning. Copyright © 2009 by Capstone. Reprinted by permission of Capstone Publishers.

Excerpt from "The Saga of Pecos Bill" from *American Folklore, Legends, and Tall Tales for Readers Theatre* by Anthony D. Fredericks. Copyright © 2008 by Anthony D. Fredericks. Reprinted by permission of the Copyright Clearance Center on behalf of Libraries Unlimited Inc.

Scaredy Squirrel by Mélanie Watt. Copyright © 2006 Mélanie Watt. Reprinted by permission of Kids Can Press Ltd., Toronto, Canada.

Excerpt from *Soccer Shootout* by Jake Maddox/Bob Temple. Text copyright © 2008 by Capstone. Reprinted by permission of Capstone Publishers.

Stink and the Freaky Frog Freakout by Megan McDonald, illustrated by Peter H. Reynolds. Text copyright © 2013 by Megan McDonald. Illustrations copyright © 2013 by Peter H. Reynolds. Reprinted by permission of the publisher, Candlewick Press and Brilliance Audio.

The U.S. Constitution by Norman Pearl, illustrated by Matthew Skeens. Copyright © 2007 by Picture Window Books. Reprinted by permission of Capstone Press Publishers.

The Upside Down Boy by Juan Felipe Herrera, illustrated by Elizabeth Gómez. Text copyright © 2000 by Juan Felipe Herrera. Illustrations copyright © 2000 by Elizabeth Gómez. Reprinted by permission of Children's Book Press, an imprint of Lee & Low Books Inc.

Why is the Statue of Liberty Green? by Martha E. H. Rustad, illustrated by Holli Conger. Copyright © 2015 by Lerner Publishing Group, Inc. Reprinted by permission of Millbrook Press, a division of Lerner Publishing Group, Inc.

Credits

10-11 (bg) ©TomasSereda/iStock/Getty Images Plus/Getty Images; 11 (super hero) ©RichVintage/E+/Getty Images; 14-15 ©Tiffany Bryant/Shutterstock; 16 (bl) ©HMH/Josh Biggs; 38 (bl) ©Michele McDonald/Candlewick Press; 58 (bl) ©Candlewick Press; 74 (bl) ©Jesus Aranguren/Houghton Mifflin Harcourt; 100 ©wavebreakmedia/Shutterstock; 103 ©VStock/Alamy Images; 108 (tr) ©vivat/Shutterstock; 108 (c) ©S. Bachstroem/Shutterstock; 108 (emoticons within text messages) ©denisgorelkin/iStock/Getty Images Plus/Getty Images; 108-109 (bg) ©Dimitri Otis/Photographer's Choice/Getty Images; 110 (bl) ©Photos.com/Getty Images; 144 (Cassie Hermansson) ©Colin Braley/Houghton Mifflin Harcourt; 147 (open journal) ©Comstock/Getty Images; 147 (quilt pattern) ©Sam Dudgeon/Houghton Mifflin Harcourt; 147 (ribbon) ©Houghton Mifflin Harcourt; 147 (blanket detail) ©ivanastar/E+/Getty Images; 147 (green cotton texture) ©Zerbor/Shutterstock; 147 (marker highlights) ©samui/Shutterstock; ©Zerbor/Shutterstock; 147 (cloth texture) ©siro46/Shutterstock; 147 (floral wallpaper pattern) ©smash338/Shutterstock; 147 (colorful sheets of felts) ©Houghton Mifflin Harcourt; 147 (burlap fabric) ©Houghton Mifflin Harcourt; 154 (bl) ©Josh Edelson/Houghton Mifflin Harcourt; 178 (bl) ©Josh Reynolds/Houghton Mifflin Harcourt; 214 ©Nick Clements/Digital Vision/Getty Images; 217 ©Getty Images; 218-219 (fireworks) ©Bailey-Cooper Photography/Alamy; 218-219 ©Joel Carillet/iStock/Getty Images Plus/Getty Images; 238-239 (bg) ©Steve Kelley/Moment/Getty Images; 238 (bl) ©Ian Dagnall/Alamy; 240 (United States of America flag detail) ©IrisImages/iStock/Getty Images Plus/Getty Images; 240 (bl) ©traveler1116/iStock/Getty Images Plus/Getty Images; 242 ©GaryBrown/iStock/Getty Images Plus/Getty Images; 243 (Betsy Ross USA flag) ©mitchellpictures/iStock/Getty Images Plus/Getty Images; 244 (bl) ©Preston Ehrler/Houghton Mifflin Harcourt; 268 (Martha E. H. Rustad) ©Andy Clayton King/Houghton Mifflin Harcourt; 286 ©Syda Productions/Shutterstock; 289 ©Blend Images/Alamy Images; 290-219 (blurred person and stage curtain) ©Marco Kesseler/Alamy; 291 (actress in mouse costume) ©aerogondo/Adobe Stock; 294 (person with script in one hand and raising other hand) ©Jupiterimages/Getty Images; 294-295 (stage curtain detail) ©Markus Pfaff/Shutterstock; 249-295 (light bulbs) ©Florian Ruppert/EyeEm/Getty Images; 294-295 (actress in costume raising hand) ©PA Images/Alamy; 296 (bl) ©Amar and Isabelle Guillen - Guillen Photo LLC/Alamy; 310-311 Jason Langley/AWL Images/Getty Images; 310 (bl) ©DESCAMPS Simon/Hemis/Alamy; 312 ©Robert Wyatt/Alamy; 314 ©Stefano Ravera/Alamy; 315 (candelabra) ©Veronika Surovtseva/Alamy; 352 ©wavebreakmedia/Shutterstock; 355 ©Fuse/Getty Images; 356-357 ©Hero Images/Dissolve Corp.; 360 (tl) ©Cosmin Iftode/Dreamstime; 360 (tr) ©monkeybusinessimages/iStock/Getty Images; 360 (cl) ©monkeybusinessimages/iStock/Getty Images Plus/